# For the Record 1997:

# *The UN Human Rights System*

## Volume 1:

# THEMATIC APPROA

# Human Rights Internet (HRI)

Founded in 1976, Human Rights Internet (HRI) is a world leader in the exchange of information within the worldwide human rights community. An international non-governmental organization (NGO) based in Ottawa, Canada, HRI has consultative status with the Economic and Social Council (ECOSOC) of the United Nations and with UNICEF and observer status with the African Commission on Human and Peoples' Rights.

On the premise that accurate information is a precondition for the effective protection of human rights, HRI's primary role is to serve the information needs of international scholars, human rights activists, asylum lawyers, and other organizations via an extensive documentation centre, computerized databases, and a Website on the internet. HRI also serves the information needs of the international human rights community with an active and extensive publications program, which includes regular publications (such as HRI's quarterly *Human Rights Tribune)*, human rights directories, and special or occasional publications. A key objective of HRI is to support the work of the global non-governmental community in its struggle to obtain human rights for all. To this end, HRI promotes human rights education, stimulates research, encourages the sharing of information, and builds international solidarity among those committed to the principles enshrined in the International Bill of Human Rights.

This report was produced by Human Rights Internet (HRI) in partnership with the Human Rights Division of the Department of Foreign Affairs and International Trade, Ottawa, Canada. The International Advisory Committee which assisted in the production of this report included: Peter Burns, Professor of Law at the University of British Columbia, a member of the UN Committee against Torture; Jane Connors, Chief of the Women's Rights Unit of the UN Division for the Advancement of Women; Osamu Shiraishi, Office of the UN High Commissioner for Human Rights; and Nicole Rivard-Royer, Policy Branch, Canadian International Development Agency (CIDA).

For further information, contact:

**Human Rights Internet**

8 York St., Suite 302

Ottawa, ON K1N 5S6

Canada

Tel: (1-613) 789-7407

Fax: (1-613) 789-7414

E-mail: hri@hri.ca

URL: http://www.hri.ca

# Table of Contents
# Volume 1 — Thematic Approaches

# Table of Contents
## Volume 2 — Africa

# Table of Contents
## Volume 3 — Asia

# Table of Contents
## Volume 4 — Latin America and the Caribbean

# Table of Contents
## Volume 5 — Eastern Europe

# Table of Contents
# Volume 6 — Western Europe and Other

# GLOSSARY OF ACRONYMS

| | |
|---|---|
| **CAT** | Committee Against Torture |
| **CCPR** | Committee on Civil and Political Rights, also known as the Human Rights Committee (HRC) |
| **CEDAW** | Committee on the Elimination of Discrimination Against Women |
| **CERD** | Committee on the Elimination of Racial Discrimination |
| **CESCR** | Committee on Economic, Social and Cultural Rights |
| **CHR** | Commission on Human Rights |
| **CRC** | Committee on the Rights of the Child |
| **DAW** | Division for the Advancement of Women |
| **CSW** | Commission on the Status of Women |
| **ECOSOC** | Economic and Social Council |
| **GA** | General Assembly |
| **HRC** | Human Rights Committee, also known as the Committee on Civil and Political Rights (CCPR) |
| **ICJ** | International Court of Justice |
| **SC** | Security Council |
| **S-G** | Secretary-General |
| **SR** | Special Rapporteur |
| **Spec Rep** | Special Representative |
| **UDHR** | Universal Declaration of Human Rights |
| **UN** | United Nations |
| **UNHCHR** | United Nations High Commissioner for Human Rights |
| **UNHCR** | United Nations High Commissioner for Refugees |
| **WG** | Working Group |

# *Preface*
# *by the Minister of Foreign Affairs*

The 50th Anniversary of the Universal Declaration of Human Rights is an occasion to commemorate and reaffirm a historic commitment undertaken by members of the international community. When, in 1948, the member states of the United Nations Assembly adopted the Declaration, they moved to enshrine once and for all the fundamental rights of the individual human being wherever she or he may live.

From that day forward, human rights were to be as central to life as food, water, air and shelter. People were no longer to be denied the right to life, liberty and security, nor to freedom of thought, conscience and religion. The Declaration was proclaimed as the "common standard of achievement for all peoples and all nations."

The Declaration is a milestone document for humanity. It has set the direction of all ensuing work in the area of human rights. In 1982, Canada developed its own Charter of Rights and Freedoms based on the principles of the Declaration. The Canadian Charter reflects values that are important to Canadians such as justice, fairness, tolerance and mutual respect.

But the struggle for the universal application and promotion of the principles of the Declaration is far from over. While the concept of human rights and the need for governments to respect them is now widespread, the continuing abuses of human rights in many parts of the world demonstrate that their universality is still not fully accepted. Respect for human rights must not be taken for granted. We must remain vigilant to ensure that they are universally and constantly promoted, protected and advanced — both in Canada and around the world.

This campaign is not for governments alone, but for all members of society whatever their compact, be they civil, judicial, religious or political. To this end, and as a special Canadian contribution to this commemorative anniversary of the Universal Declaration, it gives me great pleasure to join in partnership with civil society in the production of this first annual report on the work of the United Nations Human Rights system.

Based solely on UN documents, this report will provide in one place all the relevant information about the human rights situation in every country around the world as discussed and examined in the United Nations human rights fora. Its intent is to simplify, encourage and improve human rights policy-making. It will provide a concise, readily available information and reference source to researchers, academics, civil servants, diplomats, lawyers, human rights activists, journalists and others who work to promote and protect universal human rights.

Above all, I welcome this report as a further contribution by Canada and Canadians to nurture and strengthen the universal commitment undertaken by those member states 50 years ago at the United Nations. We must ensure that human rights remain an important part of our legacy to future generations, both nationally and internationally.

Lloyd Axworthy
Minister of Foreign Affairs

# *Foreword by*
# *the UN High Commissioner for Human Rights*

In 1998, as we commemorate the 50th Anniversary of the Universal Declaration, the international community is challenged to renew its commitment to make the message of the Declaration a part of every person's daily life. The theme for the year, "All Human Rights for All," guides many initiatives being undertaken worldwide to raise human rights awareness through education and dissemination of information. I welcome these initiatives in the belief that full knowledge of human rights empowers people and indeed is the prerequisite for the enjoyment and effective defence of their basic human rights. These initiatives will also lead to the advancement of a global human rights culture — a major tool in shaping conditions not only for the full development of individuals but also for mutual respect and understanding between peoples and countries.

The international community, unfortunately, cannot take pride in its global human rights record. At the dawn of the 21st century, we continue to encounter formidable challenges including widespread poverty and famine, underdevelopment, inadequate health care and education systems, millions of refugees and internally displaced persons, violence against women and children, racial discrimination, summary executions and torture: all illustrative of the obstacles still to be overcome. No country's human rights record is perfect. Improvements are both possible and necessary in every part of the globe. Yet, there is a sound basis for hope. I see a growing worldwide movement for human rights; a renewed dedication to eradicating serious human rights violations and a willingness of countries to take ownership of the issue of their own human rights and to address internal capacity building. Governments and non-governmental organizations, regional and international organizations are joining their efforts in advocacy of human rights. Within the United Nations, following the call by the World Conference on Human Rights and under the leadership of the Secretary-General Kofi Annan, human rights are being mainstreamed in all the programmes and activities of the Organization.

I am pleased that during this anniversary year, considerable emphasis is being placed on the work of the United Nations in promoting and protecting human rights. I believe we will be able to make this work more effective with the support of all those who care. Our major goal is to assist governments and civil society in their efforts to promote and protect human rights. Activities of the United Nations human rights machinery, which includes intergovernmental and independent expert bodies, are of paramount importance to this end. On the initiative of the Government of Canada and with its support, Human Rights Internet has prepared the present volume, which contains a review of action undertaken by the machinery relating to human rights developments at the national level. I hope that this valuable publication, an important contribution to the commemoration of the 50th Anniversary of the Universal Declaration, will also bring about wider understanding of the work of the United Nations.

Mary Robinson
Geneva, 18 May 1998

# *Introduction*

## The UN's Record in the Field of Human Rights

For over five decades, the United Nations has been actively engaged in the promotion and protection of human rights. The first concrete result of its work was the adoption, on December 9, 1948, of the first multilateral human rights treaty, the Convention on the Prevention and Punishment of the Crime of Genocide. The following day, the General Assembly adopted the Universal Declaration of Human Rights (UDHR), which has become the cornerstone of the international protection system. The first two decades of UN action were devoted almost exclusively to the promotion and elaboration of international human rights standards. There currently exist close to one hundred treaties that form the corpus of international human rights law, most of them elaborated under the aegis of the UN. At the core of this body of law are the two International Covenants, the first on economic, social and cultural rights, and the second on civil and political rights, which represent the elaboration and codification of the rights set out in the UDHR.

Beginning in the late 1960's, when the two covenants were adopted, the UN cautiously began to move into the area of protection, initially by doing in-depth studies of situations where gross violations of human rights were alleged to be occurring. Over the next three decades, the UN developed an elaborate set of procedures and mechanisms for monitoring and taking action with respect to human rights violations. In the Commission on Human Rights (CHR) — the intergovernmental body constituted in 1946 as one of the functional commissions of the UN Economic and Social Council — violations were discussed under either the confidential 1503 procedure, or under the public 1235 procedure whereby the CHR gave annual consideration to the question of violations of human rights and fundamental freedoms. The Sub-Commission on Prevention of Discrimination and Protection of Minorities, an expert body established by the CHR in 1947, supplemented the work of the Commission. The 1980s saw the establishment of a series of mechanisms, which included country-specific or thematic Working Groups, Special Rapporteurs, Special Representatives, or Independent Experts with mandates to monitor compliance by governments and to protect victims (or potential victims) of human rights abuses. These mechanisms began to generate annual reports on countries in crisis or on such critical problems as disappearances, torture, extrajudicial execution, arbitrary detention, freedom of expression, freedom of religion, the sale of children, or violence against women.

Parallel to this has been another development: since 1976, when the two international Covenants gained enough ratifications to enter into force, the treaty-body system came into being. There are now six international human rights treaties (the two international Covenants and the Conventions on the elimination of racial discrimination, the elimination of discrimination against women, torture, and the rights of the child) which have created expert bodies to which States Parties are required to periodically report. Specifically, governments are required to present written reports to these treaty bodies and then to dialogue with the experts on measures they have taken to implement the provisions of the treaty, as well as obstacles they face in this regard. In addition, three of the above-mentioned treaties — on civil and political rights, racial discrimination and torture — provided that States Parties may recognize the competence of the treaty body to receive communications from, and act with respect to, citizens alleging violations of their human rights (as elaborated in that treaty) by their governments. In some cases, the treaty bodies (sometimes in conjunction with the Special Rapporteurs of the Commission on Human Rights) have also developed an urgent action response mechanism when alerted to individuals at risk (e.g., of torture, execution, arbitrary detention, etc.)

Most recently, since the establishment of the Office of the High Commissioner for Human Rights in 1994, we have also seen UN field missions or field presences actively engaged in human rights monitoring in countries such as Rwanda, the former Yugoslavia, Haiti and Cambodia. Supplementing this has been the provision of technical assistance to governments in the area of human rights, in law reform, in training the police and the judiciary in human rights standards, or in strengthening civil society institutions.

Finally, since the Vienna World Conference on Human Rights in June 1993 — when a consensus was forged reaffirming the basic principles set out in the Universal Declaration of Human Rights, acknowledging that "the promotion and protection of all human rights is a legitimate concern of the international community", and emphasizing that "all human rights are universal, indivisible and interdependent and interrelated" there has been a concerted effort to begin a process of integrating human rights into the work of all UN bodies and throughout the UN system.

**Why This Report?**

Despite this substantial record, much of the UN's action in the field of human rights is largely unknown outside the walls of the Palais des Nations in Geneva (where most of the human rights meetings take place) or UN headquarters in New York. There are a number of reasons for this. Until recently, UN human rights documents were difficult to obtain. If you were outside Geneva or New York, either you got the documents by attending the meeting in question, or you went to a library which served as a UN depository and requested the material, preferably by document number. Not surprisingly, accessing such material was far more difficult in countries of the developing South than it was in countries of the industrialized North.

Since December 10, 1996, when the Office of the High Commissioner for Human Rights opened its Home Page on the World Wide Web, there has been a dramatic improvement in our ability to access UN human rights documentation. For example, it is now possible to get many documents of the Commission on Human Rights by going on-line and down-loading them, well before the Commission begins its work in March. As well, a very substantial part of UN documentation can now be obtained by accessing the UN's Optical Disk System on the Internet for an annual subscription fee of $1,500 US.

Nonetheless, even with access to the Internet, getting country-specific information about UN action in the field of human rights involves visiting a plethora of different Web pages to locate the critical documents needed. Thus, a key purpose of this volume is to pull together all relevant UN documents about the human rights situation in every country, so that the information is readily accessible to governments, NGOs, researchers, journalists and others. The hope is that this will facilitate informed policy-making in the area of human rights, whether by governmental, inter-governmental or non-governmental actors. In addition, the report has a thematic section which summarizes the major developments that occurred in the UN arena concerning human rights during the last calendar year (1997).

**Format**

The report is produced in three formats: in hardcopy (in English and French); on the World Wide Web, with full hyperlinks to all the original documentation for the English report; and as a CD-ROM (of the Website) for dissemination in the South.

It is important to stress that, while we must of necessity summarize actions and decisions of UN bodies and mechanisms, we have striven to present the material as objectively as possible, and with no editorial comment.

The time-period covered by the report is the calendar year, from 1 January to 31 December 1997. The focus is on the main bodies that take action in the area of human rights. In concrete terms, this means that we cover the work of the Commission on Human Rights in March/April, the Sub-Commission in August, ECOSOC in July, the Third Committee of the General Assembly in November, the sessions of the treaty-bodies whenever they meet throughout the year, and actions or decisions of the Security Council and UN field presences whenever these are relevant. In future years, we hope to expand the coverage to encompass the work of other bodies and agencies in the UN system. However, for this initial report, we have focused narrowly on the major areas of activity.

Because of its size, the report is being presented in six volumes to make it more manageable for those who will want the report close at hand when they attend relevant UN meetings. Vol. 1 (which includes this introduction) also contains: the Thematic Section of the report; an Appendix describing UN bodies and mechanisms; a calendar indicating when treaty-bodies plan to consider the reports of specific countries; and a list indicating when the different mechanisms of the Commission on Human Rights are up for renewal. The other volumes are geographically organized: Vol. 2, Africa; Vol. 3, Asia; Vol. 4, Latin America and the Caribbean; Vol. 5, Eastern Europe, and Vol. 6., Western Europe and Other.

**Partnership and Acknowledgements**

The report has been produced by Human Rights Internet (HRI) — an international NGO in consultative status with ECOSOC, headquartered in Ottawa, Canada — in partnership with the Canadian Department of Foreign Affairs and International Trade (DFAIT). The research, writing and editing, as well as the development of the Website, was done by a small HRI team. The team worked closely with the Human Rights Division of DFAIT and under the guidance of an international advisory committee that included individuals knowledgeable about the Office of the High Commissioner for Human Rights and the HCHR's Website, the UN Division for the Advancement of Women, the treaty bodies, DFAIT and the Canadian International Development Agency (CIDA). This notwithstanding, Human Rights Internet alone assumes responsibility for any errors in fact or judgment found in this report.

Work on this report began in August, with the bulk of it completed within a six-month period. This would not have been possible without the indefatigable Jan Bauer, who wrote the draft manuscript, and a team of three interns (Britt Elliott, Cynthia Gervais and Paul Williams, later joined by a fourth, Steve Mason) who amassed and prepared all the documentation to be summarized. Tanja Kisslinger, HRI's Website Coordinator, is responsible for the design and execution of the Website, and for supervising the HTML coding of thousands of pages of documentation.

Ross Hynes and Adele Dion, successively directors of the Human Rights Division of DFAIT, were responsible for ensuring the life of the report, while Robert Lawrence assumed the unenviable position of coordinating the project. The fact that this report has become a reality is due, in large part, to the vision and commitment of the Honourable Lloyd Axworthy, Canada's Minister of Foreign Affairs.

Laurie Wiseberg
Executive Director
Human Rights Internet

# Overview: 1997

This thematic section of *For the Record* is intended to highlight major developments in the United Nations human rights system during 1997. In this pilot issue, no attempt has been made to be exhaustive in reviewing all developments. Instead, we have focussed largely on the thematic mechanisms of the Commission on Human Rights, key reports and resolutions of the Sub-Commission, and General Comments of the treaty-bodies.

Nonetheless, a number of critical developments are not captured through these lens, the following among them.

On March 15, 1997, the first UN High Commissioner for Human Rights (UNHCHR), Mr. José Ayala Lasso, resigned to take up an appointment as Foreign Minister of Ecuador. The General Assembly had established the post of UNHCHR, tasked with coordinating human rights work throughout the United Nations system, in February 1994, following a strong recommendation in the Vienna Declaration and Plan of Action (VDPA) adopted at the World Conference on Human Rights, June 1993. Mr. Ayala Lasso had held the post since 5 April 1994.

On 12 September 1997, Ms. Mary Robinson, former President of Ireland, became the second High Commissioner for Human Rights. Secretary-General Kofi Anan subsequently announced the appointment of Mr. Enrique ter Horst of Venezuela as her Deputy.

A major restructuring of the human rights secretariat also took place in 1997 with a merger of the UN Centre for Human Rights and the High Commissioner's office in Geneva, now renamed the Office of the High Commissioner for Human Rights. As well, the five branches of the former Centre were reorganized into three divisions, with all staff positions reclassified.

There was substantial progress in 1997 on the drafting of a treaty and statute for an International Criminal Court (ICC), with meetings of the Third Preparatory Committee in February, the Fourth PrepCom in August and the Fifth in December. The year ended with considerable optimism that a permanent ICC will emerge from the Diplomatic Conference of Plenipotentiaries on the Establishment of an International Criminal Court (ICC) to take place in June/July 1998 in Rome, Italy.

In 1997, the International Criminal Tribunal (ICT) for the former Yugoslavia, sitting in The Hague, undertook two new trials: the Celbici case and the Blaskic case, with indictments for grave breaches of the 1949 Geneva Conventions, violations of the laws or customs of war and crimes against humanity. Both trials are ongoing. On 14 July 1997, Dusko Tadic, found guilty after a two year trial, was sentenced to 20 years' imprisonment. Both the defense and the prosecution have appealed, the latter challenging certain decisions of the judges. The ICT issued one further indictment in 1997, to Simo Drljaca and Milan Kovacevic for genocide, bringing the total number of indictments issued by the Tribunal to 20 and the total number of indictees to 74. In 1997, six new judges were elected, along with a new President (Judge Gabrielle Kirk McDonald) and Vice President. The outgoing President addressed the UN General Assembly on 4 November 1997. He identified the failure of states to arrest indictees as a major stumbling block to judicial action and appealed for all Member States to lend support to the ICT. Two major developments in 1997 were the establishment of a new code of professional conduct for the defense counsel and the recognition that the Tribunal has the authority and power to issue orders to states, who are under clear obligation to comply with them.

In January 1997, Secretary-General Kofi Annan issued a highly critical report of the International Criminal Tribunal for Rwanda (ICR), with accusations of mismanagement of funds, nepotism and corruption. As a measure to improve the workings of the court, he dismissed a number of senior administrators and put a new team in place headed by Agwu Ukiwe Okali as registrar. The first trial of the International Criminal Tribunal (ICT) for Rwanda — the trial of Jean Paul Akayesu — began in January 1997. He is charged with genocide, inciting genocide, crimes against humanity, murder, rape and sexual torture, and his trial is still on-going. The initial indictment had not included rape and sexual torture. On June 17, 1997, that the Prosecutor announced that the indictment against Akayesu would be amended to include charges of rape and other crimes of sexual violence, an amendment precipitated by the filing of an *amicus curiae* ("friend of the court") brief before the ICTR on behalf of women's groups from Rwanda and around the world. Previous to this revised indictment, none of the approximately 21 indictments issued by the ICTR had included any rape or sexual assault charges, despite reports by several non-governmental organizations (NGOs) that Rwandan women were subjected to violence on a massive scale during the 1994 genocide.

In Ottawa, Canada, from 2 to 4 December 1997, governments met to sign a treaty implementing a total ban on the production, use or stockpiling of anti-personnel landmines. This was the culmination of the Ottawa process initiated by Canadian Foreign Affairs Minister Lloyd Axworthy in October 1996, which involved non-governmental organizations, especially the International Coalition to Ban Landmines (ICBL), and like-minded governments working together in close partnership for their common objective. The final text of the *Convention on the Prohibition of the Use, Stockpiling, Production and Transfer of Anti-Personnel Mines* and on their Destruction had been adopted in Oslo on 17 September, approved by delegates from 89 countries. The ICBL and its Coordinator, Jody Williams, received the Nobel Peace Prize for their work on this issue.

# *Thematic Mechanisms and Approaches*

## CHILDREN

**Special Rapporteur on the sale of children, child prostitution, child pornography** (E/CN.4/1997/95; A/52/482)

The mandate of the Special Rapporteur (SR) on the sale of children, child prostitution and child pornography was established by the Commission in 1991 and incorporated into the work of the question of the adoption of children for commercial purposes. In 1997, the SR was Mrs. O. Calcetas-Santos (Philippines).

The 1997 report included a review of concerns in the areas of causes, characteristics, victims and abusers, and effects on children. Commentary is included on legislative developments, programmes and initiatives, analysis of the causes and problems *in situ*, an inventory of resources, priorities related to strategies for action, problem areas in the justice system and proposals for follow-up to the World Congress against Commercial Sexual Exploitation of Children. The report noted a number of positive developments concerning the protection of children from forms of abuse that fall within the mandate of the SR. Among these developments are:

▸ increasing introduction by states of laws that are distinct from assistance provided under the general category of children in need and improved protection of child victims of sexual abuse and exploitation;

▸ a growing trend to increase penalties against abusers of children and to explore punitive measures other than imprisonment;

▸ the strengthening of police powers in some countries regarding child prostitution and pornography, including arrest without warrant and sting operations;

▸ wider acceptance of extradition of offenders and extraterritorial exercise of jurisdiction;

▸ increased emphasis on advocacy and prevention campaigns and reintegration and monitoring projects; and

▸ increased interest in prevention, including a higher use of education and media to inform children and the general public.

In terms of areas that require substantial improvements, the report made special mention of the justice system, noting that in many countries the system handles cases with insensitivity and contributes to the revictimization of the child or children concerned. The report also identifies problem areas related to law enforcement, prosecution, court procedures and recovery and reintegration.

Recommendations for action at the national level, included that states:

▸ institute regular training and sensitization programmes for specialized police officers dealing with child victims, adopting a victim-centred approach;

▸ prepare a police manual on procedures for handling children, to avoid re-victimization during the investigation process;

▸ if required, initiate reform against corruption and inefficiency within the police force to restore public confidence;

▸ establish operational mobile units for the surveillance of places where children are at greater risk;

▸ ensure effective enforcement of laws aimed at protecting children by, *inter alia*, providing incentives to law enforcement officials and encouraging cooperation with non-governmental community-based organizations; and

▸ involve the community and encourage its active participation in the law enforcement process, especially in monitoring abuse and exploitation of children.

Recommendations related to criminal proceedings, included that: courts give child victims pseudonyms to conceal their identity; records such as negatives, audio tapes and photographs be destroyed subject only to exceptions ordered by the court, and those not destroyed be sealed and not made available without the permission of the court; and, sight-separation procedures be observed during hearings through, for example, the use of one-way closed circuit television testimony.

Recommendations at the international level called on all states to:

▸ determine priority countries with which closer cooperation is needed to prevent trafficking in children;

▸ explore with these countries possibilities related to: synchronization of laws on the elements of crime against children, the nature and length of penalties that can be imposed, and rules of procedure, particularly in evidence gathering; arrangements by which abusers in a foreign country may be subject to prosecution either where the offence took place or in the country of the offender; negotiation and application of multilateral conventions in regions that share a similar political, legal and social system; and submission of requests for mutual judicial assistance in criminal matters;

▸ develop a quick and accurate exchange of information between law enforcement agencies and the judiciary internationally;

- set up a central registry for missing children to facilitate the identification and tracing of child victims;

- exchange lists of paedophiles between different countries to prevent the repetition of offences by the same persons;

- coordinate efforts more closely between police, customs and postal officials to curb the circulation of pornographic materials; and,

- establish consultations and the exchange of training programmes among law enforcement authorities to deal with transnational trafficking in children.

- The commentary on follow-up to the World Congress against Commercial Sexual Exploitation of Children (Stockholm, 1996) endorsed recommendations similar to those above on international cooperation. It also focussed on the need to mobilize the business sector, including the tourism industry, and the media, against the use of its networks and establishments for the commercial sexual exploitation of children.

The SR's interim report to the General Assembly included some commentary on country-specific situations and a special section on the media and education. Information is provided on, for example, the international legal framework for the protection of children, facets of the media, the role of the press in the reporting of sexual offences, the impact of audio and radio, the print media, and pornography on-line and the Internet.

In the area of media and education, the SR recommended that, *inter alia*:

- laws for the protection of children against commercial sexual exploitation be publicized and popularized;

- prominent visibility be given to convictions of child sex offenders;

- a culture of rights and positive moral values for society be promoted, including respect for all human rights, principles for good parenthood, and, elimination of practices based on culture and tradition which are inimical to children;

- children be sensitized and educated to detect and identify aberrant behaviour and risk factors or situations making them vulnerable to commercial sexual exploitation;

- the public be educated on the pernicious and long-lasting consequences of any form of sexual abuse or exploitation of children;

- steps be taken to raise awareness among leaders of mass communications and entertainment industries related to the needs of children and the protection of their rights;

- free and compulsory primary and secondary education be provided for children;

- mechanisms for reporting crimes against children be widely publicized;

- media and education personnel be sensitized to the dangers of revictimization of children and safeguards be provided to avoid such dangers;

- training programmes for all those involved with children be designed and implemented, aimed at early detection of signs of physical or sexual abuse;

- free counselling services be offered for child victims and their families to ensure reintegration; and,

- the private sector, including computer industries, be mobilized in the fight against the commercial sexual exploitation of children through, for example, making hotlines available to enable users to report potentially harmful materials on the Internet in an effort to promote self-regulatory controls.

Renewal of the mandate will be considered by the Commission at its 1998 session.

**Omnibus Resolution of the Commission on Human Rights**

In 1997, the Commission continued its recent practice of adopting by consensus an omnibus resolution (1997/78), incorporating a number of subjects relevant to children's human rights and to the elaboration of optional protocols to the Convention on the Rights of the Child. The Commission, *inter alia*:

**Preamble:** expressed concern over the situation of children resulting from poverty, inadequate social and economic conditions, natural disasters, armed conflicts, displacement, economic and sexual exploitation, illiteracy, hunger, intolerance and disability and inadequate legal protection; and reaffirmed that the best interest of the child is the primary consideration in all action concerning children.

**I. Implementation of the Convention on the Rights of the Child:** welcomed the nearly universal ratification of the Convention; called on states parties to implement fully the provisions of the Convention, withdraw reservations incompatible with its objects and purpose and review remaining reservations; called on states parties, organs and bodies of the UN, intergovernmental and non-governmental organizations, the media and the community at large to make the principles and provisions of the Convention widely known and encourage training on the rights of the child for those involved in activities affecting children; encouraged the Committee on the Rights of the Child to continue to pay attention to the needs of children in especially difficult circumstances, including children with disabilities.

**II. The girl child:** called on states to institute legal reforms to ensure equal enjoyment by girls of all human rights and freedoms and take effective action against violations of those rights and freedoms; called on states and international and non-governmental organizations to develop and implement gender-sensitive strategies to address the rights and needs of children, take into account the particular needs of girls, especially in education, health and nutrition, and eliminate negative cultural attitudes and practices against girls; called on states to eliminate all forms of discrimination against girls and the root causes of son preference, and to protect girls from violence, including female infanticide and prenatal sex selection, genital mutilation, incest, sexual abuse and exploitation; called on states to develop age-appropriate, safe and confidential programs, and medical, social and psychological support services to assist girls who are subjected to violence.

**III. Prevention and eradication of the sale of children, and of their sexual exploitation and abuse, including child prostitution and child pornography:** welcomed the reports of the Special Rapporteur and the Working Group elaborating a draft optional protocol to the Convention on the Rights of the Child to address the issue of sale of children, child prostitution and child pornography; welcomed measures taken by governments to implement the Programme of Action for the Prevention of the Sale of Children, Child Prostitution and Child Pornography; welcomed the adoption and dissemination of the Declaration and Agenda for Action of the World Congress against Commercial Sexual Exploitation of Children; called on states to develop, implement and enforce measures to eliminate the sale of children and their sexual exploitation; called on states to criminalize commercial and all other forms of sexual exploitation of children and ensure that child victims are not penalized for such practices; called for cooperation and concerted action by all relevant law enforcement authorities and institutions and for the allocation of resources for rehabilitation of child victims of trafficking and sexual exploitation; requested the Working Group on the optional protocol to meet for two weeks (less if possible) prior to the 1998 session of the Commission to finalize the draft optional protocol before the 10th anniversary of the Convention on the Rights of the Child.

**IV. Protection of children affected by armed conflict:** welcomed the final report of the Expert of the Secretary-General and welcomed the General Assembly recommendation to appoint a Special Representative on the impact of armed conflict on children; welcomed the report of the Working Group on the draft optional protocol on the involvement of children in armed conflict; called on states to consider acceding to relevant international human rights and humanitarian law instruments and to implement those to which they are parties; called on states to participate constructively in negotiations on the optional protocol with the aim of early agreement on a text; called on states to integrate into military programs, including those for peacekeeping, instruction on responsibilities towards civilian populations, particularly women and children; called on states and other parties to armed conflict to respect international humanitarian law, end the use of children as soldiers, and ensure their demobilization and reintegration into society, including victims of land mines and other weapons, and child victims of gender-based violence; reaffirmed that rape in the conduct of armed conflict is a war crime and may constitute a crime against humanity and an act of genocide; called on states to protect all women and children from gender-based violence, including rape, sexual exploitation and forced pregnancy, and to strengthen mechanisms to investigate and prosecute perpetrators; reaffirmed that humanitarian responses in conflict situations should emphasize the special reproductive health needs of women and girls; reaffirmed the importance of preventive measures such as early-warning, preventive diplomacy and education for peace to prevent conflicts; reaffirmed support for the recommendations of General Assembly and the International Committee of the Red Cross related to the assessment and monitoring of the consequences of sanctions upon children, as well as those related to humanitarian relief; requested the Working Group on the optional protocol to meet for two weeks prior to the 1998 session of the Commission in order to finalize the draft optional protocol; invited all relevant and interested parties to cooperate with the prospective special representative of the Secretary-General on the impact of armed conflict on children.

**V. Refugee and internally displaced children:** called on states to protect refugee and internally displaced children, including through policies for care, well-being and development; called for early identification and registration of unaccompanied refugee and internally displaced children, for priority to be given to family tracing and reunification, and for continued care for unaccompanied children; called for other parties to armed conflict to recognize the particular vulnerability of refugee and internally displaced children to recruitment into armed forces and sexual violence, exploitation and abuse; stressed the special vulnerability of child-headed households and called for all concerned to give these situations urgent attention; called on states and all relevant parties to involve women and youth in the design, delivery and monitoring of measures for their protection against sexual violence and recruitment of children into armed forces.

**VI. Elimination of exploitation of child labour:** welcomed measures by governments to eliminate exploitation of child labour; welcomed governmental initiatives to convene an international conference on various forms of child labour; called on states that have not yet done so to ratify and implement ILO conventions related to child labour and the minimum age for employment and eliminate all extreme forms of child labour such as forced labour, bonded labour and other forms of slavery; called on states to take the necessary measures to provide for a minimum age or ages for admission to employment, regulation of hours of work and conditions of employment, and appropriate penalties or sanctions to ensure enforcement of laws and standards; called on states to set specific target dates for the elimination of all forms of child labour that are contrary to accepted international standards, to ensure full enforcement of relevant existing laws and enact legislation necessary to implement obligations under the Convention on the Rights of the Child and ILO conventions; called on states to support the proposed drafting of an ILO instrument aimed at eradicating the most intolerable forms of child labour; requested the Secretary-General to provide information on initiatives aimed at eliminating exploitation of child labour and recommend ways and means to improve cooperation at national and international levels in this area.

**VII. The plight of street children:** called on states to continue to seek comprehensive solutions to the problems of children on the street, in conformity with obligations under relevant international human rights instruments; called on states to ensure the reintegration of street children into society and to provide them with adequate nutrition, shelter, health care and education; called on all states to take measures to prevent the killing of street children, to combat torture and violence against them, and to ensure that legal and juridical processes respect children's rights against arbitrary deprivation of liberty, maltreatment and abuse.

**VIII. The Commission decided:** to request the Secretary-General to appoint for a three-year period a Special Representative on the impact of armed conflict on children.

* * * * * * * *

# DETENTION

**Working Group on Arbitrary Detention** (E/CN.4/1997/4; E/CN.4/1997/4/Add.1)

The Working Group (WG) on Arbitrary Detention was established by the Commission in 1991 (resolution 1991/42) charged with the task of investigating cases of detention imposed arbitrarily or otherwise inconsistent with international standards set forth in relevant international instruments. The WG is composed of five independent experts. The Group's mandate is subject to renewal every three years. Cases considered by the WG are those that fall into one or more of three categories in which the deprivation of liberty or freedom is arbitrary:

1. as it manifestly cannot be linked to any legal basis (such as continued detention beyond the execution of the sentence or despite an amnesty act);

2. based on facts giving rise to prosecution or conviction related to the exercise of certain fundamental freedoms which are protected by the Universal Declaration and the International Covenant on Civil and Political Rights (the latter for states parties) and, in particular, the rights to freedom of thought, conscience and religion, freedom of opinion and expression, and the right of peaceful assembly and association; and/or

3. based on non-observance of all or part of the international provisions related to the right to fair trial to the extent that it confers on the deprivation of freedom, of whatever kind, an arbitrary character.

In the last few years, several governments have questioned the approach taken by the WG, basing their objections on the distinction between "detention" and "imprisonment" contained in the UN's Body of Principles for the Protection of All Persons under Any Form of Detention or Imprisonment. The Principles define a "detained person" as anyone "deprived of personal liberty except as a result of conviction for an offence" and an "imprisoned person" as anyone "deprived of personal liberty as a result of conviction for an offence". The governments which have questioned the WG's approach have maintained that anyone convicted under national law could not be considered detained, even in those cases where national legislation is inconsistent or violates international norms, and therefore no such case could properly be considered to fall within the mandate of the WG.

The resolution adopted at the 1996 session of the Commission (1996/28) requested the WG to take into consideration the distinction between detention and imprisonment. The WG's 1997 report includes commentary on the Group's deliberations and summarizes its conclusions, stating:

‣ it is not the intention of the Commission on Human Rights to restrict every person's right not to be arbitrarily deprived of freedom to pre-trial situations;

‣ the essence of the mandate derives from the word "arbitrary" and therefore addresses the need to eliminate, in all its forms, arbitrariness, irrespective of the phase of deprivation of liberty concerned;

‣ proceeding on the basis of a distinction between detention and imprisonment as set out in the Body of Principles

would mean that deprivations of liberty resulting in sentencing in the absence of proper guarantees of due process would no longer be prohibited under the provisions in international human rights instruments which form the foundation for the mandate of the WG;

‣ the mandate of the Group was established with reference to article 10 of the Universal Declaration, related to a fair and public hearing by an independent and impartial tribunal; thus, the Commission intended the WG to consider detentions and sentences imposed by courts that are not independent or impartial and either had not heard the accused or had not done so publicly;

‣ arbitrary deprivations of liberty are not carried out only by the judiciary and thus it was not the Commission's intention for the WG not to consider allegations and cases committed by the executive branch of government or other comparable bodies;

‣ the distinction between detention and imprisonment is only used in the Body of Principles; other texts use either term and both have been accepted by states as valid descriptions of deprivation of liberty — whether pre-trial or post-trial;

‣ the WG's mandate is not restricted to the Universal Declaration or the Body of Principles; it applies to all relevant international legal instruments accepted by the states concerned, including both conventional mechanisms and resolutions adopted by the General Assembly and the Economic and Social Council;

‣ article 9 of the Universal Declaration specifically refers to arbitrary arrest, detention and exile and therefore the Declaration condemns arbitrariness in all forms of deprivation of liberty;

‣ if detention refers only to pre-trial detention then it must be concluded that the Universal Declaration does not condemn arbitrary imprisonment following a trial of whatever nature; and

‣ the Body of Principles makes clear that the distinction drawn between detention and imprisonment is to be used only for the purposes of that text and no other; further, that the Principles do not define anything but merely establish a use of terms for the purposes of the Principles.

Thus, in considering the implications of limiting the WG's mandate to detention as defined in the Body of Principles, the Group stated that its credibility would be seriously challenged if it should express an opinion only concerning the very first days of pre-trial detention. It gave the example of a case in which a person was condemned to a heavy sentence for having written an editorial or a book; where the sentence was handed down by a special court after a secret trial, held a very short time after the arrest of the defendant; and where the rights of the defence had not been respected. The Group further stated that, were the distinction in the Principles between "detention" and "imprisonment" to prevail, it would not be able to consider the deprivation of liberty of a person who, for example, had previously been tried for the same offence or crime, and perhaps even found not guilty; or sentenced for an act which, at the time it was committed, did not constitute an offence.

The resolution adopted at the 1997 session of the Commission resolved, to some degree, the dispute over "detention" and "imprisonment" by adopting the term "arbitrary deprivation of liberty" or a variation thereof. The Commission entrusted to the WG the task of "investigating cases of deprivation of liberty imposed arbitrarily, provided that no final decision has been taken in such cases by domestic courts in conformity with: (a) domestic law; (b) relevant international standards set out in the Universal Declaration; and, (c) relevant international instruments accepted by the states concerned.

The WG reaffirmed the recommendations made in its 1996 report (E/CN.4/1996/40) in areas related to, for example, the causes of arbitrary detention and steps that could be taken to prevent or reduce them and the release of persons who have been arbitrarily detained, especially those detained for many years. The WG specifically:

▸ emphasized the need for governments to respond to cases transmitted to them within the 90-day period and provide detailed information with regard to both facts and law;

▸ requested the Commission to recommend that relevant governments lift long-standing states of emergency and restore normal rule of law and, in cases where a state of emergency is justified, to recommend that the government concerned strictly apply the principle of proportionality;

▸ suggested that the Commission request governments to eliminate from national legislation precepts sanctioning modes of conduct without describing them with sufficient clarity so that individuals may understand clearly which conduct is lawful and which is not, without possible room for doubt; and

▸ suggested that the Commission request states to incorporate the remedy of habeas corpus in national legislation, as an individual right.

The resolution adopted at the 1997 session (1997/50): reaffirmed relevant articles in the Universal Declaration and the ICCPR; noted efforts of the WG to revise its methods of work and strengthen dialogue with states; invited the WG to continue to seek and gather information from all sources, including individuals concerned, their families and legal representation; invited the WG to re-examine its methods of work and particularly those related to admissibility of communications received, urgent appeals and deadlines set for governments to reply to requests for information on individual cases; invited the WG to take gender-specificity into account in its reports and give particular attention to the situation of women subjected to arbitrary deprivation of liberty; affirmed that the WG can take up cases on its own initiative; requested that attention be given to reports concerning the situation of immigrants and asylum seekers allegedly being held in prolonged administrative custody without possibility of administrative or judicial remedy and include observations on this subject in the report to the 1998 Commission; noted the decision of the WG not to apply the ICCPR and other international legal instruments to states that are not parties to them; appealed to states that have not done so to become parties to international human rights instruments and for states parties to withdraw reservations to relevant instruments; noted the decision of the WG in future to give views rather than take decisions; requested governments to take

appropriate steps to remedy the situation of persons arbitrarily deprived of liberty and inform the WG of steps taken; encouraged governments to give attention to the recommendation of the WG related to persons detained for a number of years and ensure that national legislation is in conformity with relevant international standards and applicable legal instruments; encouraged governments not to extend states of emergency beyond what is strictly required or to limit their effects; encouraged all governments to invite the WG to their countries; requested governments concerned to give necessary attention to urgent appeals forwarded to them by the WG; and extended the mandate of the WG for three years with the task of investigating cases of deprivation of liberty imposed arbitrarily.

The mandate of the WG will be up for renewal again at the Commission's session in the year 2000.

\* \* \* \* \* \* \* \*

# DEVELOPMENT

### Group of Experts on the right to development
(E/CN.4/1997/22)

At the 1996 session, the Commission reaffirmed that the right to development is an integral part of fundamental human rights and urged states to integrate civil, cultural, economic, political and social rights into development activities. The Commission also decided to establish, for a two-year period, a ten-member intergovernmental group of experts with a mandate to elaborate a strategy for the implementation and promotion of the right to development. The Commission further expressed its expectation that the Group of Experts would consult with the human rights treaty bodies and the High Commissioner for Human Rights on all issues relevant to implementation of the right to development.

The 1997 report of the Group of Experts has two main features: commentary on the multidimensional aspects of the right to development and proposals for measures that may be undertaken in future for the implementation and promotion of the right. In terms of the multidimensional aspects, the report acknowledges that development is not only a process but also a right of all individuals, groups and peoples, which incorporates a wide range of aspects, including economic, social, cultural and political ones. Human rights mechanisms and instruments are seen as useful in promoting the development process and the whole range of human rights. The report notes that individuals, groups and peoples, particularly from disadvantaged sections of societies, should be able to exercise their rights to participate meaningfully in and enjoy the benefits of development.

The report includes a chart of issues that the Group of Experts, observer government delegations and NGOs identified as related to the right to development.

Economic aspects of the right, at the international and national levels, were seen to incorporate such issues as: trade relations, financial resources, aid resources, structural adjustment programs, technology transfer, transnational corporations, the right of states over natural wealth and resources, environmental protection, unilateral coercive economic measures, globalization, poverty eradication, public spending patterns, the right to property, land distribution and land reform, land rights and resources for indigenous peoples, trade unions, corruption and the right of states to plan development policies.

Social aspects of the right were seen to incorporate such issues as: health, housing, education, food security, employment, migration and migrant workers, refugees and asylum seekers, trafficking in children and women, trafficking in human organs, child pornography, sexual exploitation of children, social alienation (crime, violence, drugs), social and racial discrimination, the situation of vulnerable groups (e.g., persons with disabilities, the homeless, the unemployed), internally displaced persons, effects of new technologies, women's empowerment, protection of children and families and "structural violence".

The cultural aspects of the right to development were seen to include such issues as: education, language and literacy, human rights education, the media and the effects of monopolies, new information and communication technologies, cultural diversity, local and national cultures, cultural rights of minorities, protection of indigenous and local knowledge systems and customs, protection of cultural heritage, desecration of holy places, traditional practices affecting women's health, and the cultural rights of indigenous peoples and minorities.

The political and civil rights aspects of the right were seen to include such issues as: transparent and accountable government, absence of corruption and nepotism, popular participation in the development process, good governance, democracy, rule of law, equality and non-discrimination, equal protection of the law, due process, fair trial, independence of the judiciary, the right to vote and be elected, freedom of movement, freedom of assembly and association, freedom of thought, opinion and expression, genocide, a stable social order, self-determination, non-interference in the internal affairs of other states, freedom from foreign occupation or domination, extraterritorial application of domestic law, national sovereignty over natural wealth and resources, disarmament, humanitarian assistance and prevention of conflicts.

Proposals in the report on measures that might be taken in future to ensure promotion and implementation of the right to development covered a wide range of considerations. These had not, however, been discussed or adopted by the Group. They included that:

▸ ECOSOC, or a new lost-cost forum, facilitate an international dialogue with all parties to the development process and all actors involved in the implementation of human rights and the right to development;

▸ international cooperation be designed to implement the right to development as a preventive approach to international security;

▸ dialogue on the right to development and internal peace be held at the national level with all parties concerned;

▸ the right to development and human rights be introduced into the policies and programs of international institutions managing the economic world;

▸ the human rights treaty bodies integrate into their activities questions related to implementation of the right to development and address structural impediments to the enjoyment of human rights;

▸ a legal instrument on the right to development be developed, perhaps as optional protocols to the International Covenants on Human Rights, a convention on the right to development, or a framework convention incorporating legally binding principles for directing the development policies of states, introducing or reconfirming the human rights approach to development;

▸ a follow-up mechanism be created to review violations of the right to development at the national and international levels, including a voluntary reporting system based on targets and objectives to be set by each state;

▸ effects of trade rules on equity and development prospects be studied and, if necessary, adapted;

▸ measures and mechanisms be put in place to ensure an adequate net flow of financial resources to developing countries;

▸ a monitoring mechanism be established to ensure that developed countries meet the commitment to provide at least 0.7 per cent of their GDP as aid to developing countries;

▸ a larger share of aid be dedicated to the eradication of poverty and promotion of social and sustainable development;

▸ a comprehensive approach to resolving the external debt problem be adopted;

▸ a mechanism be set up to ensure that concerns related to structural adjustment programs are effectively taken into account at the time such programs are designed;

▸ a working group be established within the United Nations to address issues arising from the growing influence and impact of transnational corporations related to ethics, environment, health and safety, culture, technology transfer, effects on local firms and sectors and the domestic economy and local resources;

▸ a working group be established to examine inequities and imbalances in international economic relations;

▸ a mechanism be established to coordinate macroeconomic policies at the global level;

▸ measures be taken to ensure that human rights are not used as an instrument of trade protectionism or as leverage for narrow economic or commercial ends;

▸ measures be taken to address fears of human rights being used as a conditionality for aid, loans or trade;

▸ measures be taken to eliminate coercive economic measures and extraterritorial application of domestic laws;

▸ a mechanism be set up to examine imbalances in decision-making powers on global issues between developed and developing countries and major and smaller nations, including consideration of this question as it relates to the Bretton Woods Institutions, the World Trade Organization, the Security Council and other UN bodies;

▸ a commission or working group be established to examine and take measures to counter the adverse effects of globalization and liberalization on the development prospects of people;

▸ peace dividend resources be allocated to comprehensive development in developing countries;

▸ international cooperation be enhanced to fight drug-trafficking, trafficking in women and children, sexual exploitation and prostitution;

▸ international cooperation be enhanced to eliminate child labour;

▸ appropriate three-party mechanisms be established and developed to ensure the active participation of the entire population in the process of consultation, drafting and implementation of development programs;

▸ national coordinating committees for human rights be established;

▸ national institutions be established and/or strengthened for the promotion and protection of all human rights and especially the core human rights;

▸ national judges be obliged to apply international human rights law; and

▸ corruption be made punishable in national law.

The question of the renewal of the mandate of the Group of Experts, or the establishment of a different mechanism, was considered at the 1998 session of the Commission.

At its 1997 session, the Commission adopted a resolution on the right to development (1997/72) by consensus. The Commission, *inter alia*: notes the reaffirmation at the World Conference on Human Rights of the right to development as a universal and inalienable human right; noted that the human person is the central subject of development; emphasized that all human rights are universal, indivisible, interdependent and interrelated; underlined the fact that realization of the right to development requires effective development policies at the national level and equitable economic relations and a favourable economic environment at the international level; affirmed the need to apply a gender perspective in implementation of the right to development, including by ensuring that women play an active role in the development process; reaffirmed the importance of the right to development for every person and all peoples in all countries as an integral part of fundamental human rights; recognized that the Declaration on the Right to Development is an integral link between the Universal Declaration and the Vienna Declaration and Programme of Action through a holistic view integrating economic, social and cultural rights with civil and political rights; urged states to eliminate obstacles to development at all levels; urged all states to promote the right to development as a vital element in a balanced human rights program; requested the High Commissioner for Human Rights to provide the Declaration on the Right to Development with a profile commensurate with its importance; called on the High Commissioner to continue to give priority to the right to development and provide necessary staff, services and resources for programmatic follow-up; recommended that activities associated with the 50th anniversary of the Universal Declaration project the role and importance of the right to development; noted the dialogue initiated by the High Commissioner for Human Rights with the World Bank and stressed that the dialogue should identify obstacles to realization of the right to development, contribute to initiatives to promote the right and focus on mainstreaming a gender perspective in implementation of the Declaration; welcomed the High Commissioner's initiative to organize regional seminars on all aspects of the right to development; called on the Group of Experts to encourage participation in the work by states, international institutions and non-governmental organizations, continue elaboration of a strategy for the implementation and promotion of the right to development, continue to explore ways to promote international cooperation, dialogue and partnership for realization of the right to development, and, give due consideration to the possibility of establishing a follow-up mechanism, or enhance existing ones.

The Working Group held its second session in Geneva, 29 September–10 October 1997, focussing on the need for a global approach to the right to development and for a follow-up mechanism. Its report will be considered at the 1998 session of the CHR.

\* \* \* \* \* \* \* \*

# DISABILITIES

The Standard Rules on the Equalization of Opportunities for Persons with Disabilities were adopted by the General Assembly in 1993. The Rules stipulated that they would be monitored within the framework of the sessions of the Commission for Social Development (CSD). In March 1994, the Secretary-General appointed a Special Rapporteur (SR) for a period of three years to monitor implementation of the Standard Rules. The Rules also stipulated that, at the end of the SR's mandate, the CSD should examine the possibility of either renewing that mandate, appointing a new SR or considering another monitoring mechanism. The SR's mandate was renewed by the CSD at its 1997 session.

The SR's report, transmitted to the General Assembly with a note by the Secretary-General (A/52/56), includes commentary on, *inter alia*: activities in the UN system related to human rights and disability, and surveys undertaken by the SR in such areas as general policy, legislation, accessibility, organizations of persons with disabilities, education, legal regulation of the right to special education, the role of parents, education and the issue of integration and employment.

There is no specific mechanism at the Commission on Human Rights to address the issue of the human rights of persons with disabilities. Nonetheless, the CHR has, for a number of years, adopted a resolution on this subject. At the 1997 session, however, the Commission adopted by consensus a draft decision (1997/107) through which the question was biennualized. The text was not substantive in that it did not address violations of the human rights of persons with disabilities. The Commission simply took note of the report of the CSD's Special Rapporteur, invited the SR to present his report to the 1998 session of the CHR and decided to renew consideration of the question at the 1998 session.

\* \* \* \* \* \* \* \*

# DISAPPEARANCES

**Working Group on enforced or involuntary disappearances** (E/CN.4/1997/34)

The Working Group (WG) on Enforced or Involuntary Disappearances, established in 1980, was the first thematic mechanism set up by the Commission on Human Rights to deal with specific human rights violations of a particularly serious nature occurring on a global scale. The basic mandate, renewable every three years, is to assist relatives of disappeared persons to ascertain the fate and whereabouts of their missing family members. The cases are dealt with on a humanitarian basis, irrespective of whether the government concerned has ratified any of the existing legal instruments which provide for an individual complaints procedure. The WG acts on the principle that the state is responsible for human rights violations committed within its territory and is obligated to prevent such violations or to investigate them when they have occurred. This responsibility continues to exist irrespective of changes of government. The WG does not deal with situations of international armed conflict. Nor will it consider abductions which are not directly or indirectly attributable to a government (i.e., the Group will not process individual cases of disappearance perpetrated by irregular or insurgent groups fighting a government on its own territory). This not withstanding, the WG operates on the assumption that information on all disappearances is relevant to a proper evaluation of an overall situation. Since its establishment, the WG has dealt with some 50,000 individual cases occurring in more than 70 countries.

Following the 1992 adoption by the General Assembly of the Declaration on the Protection of All Persons from Enforced Disappearances, the WG was also given the task of monitoring states' compliance with the Declaration. The effect of the Declaration was to place states "under an obligation to take effective measures to prevent and terminate acts of enforced disappearance by making them continuing offences under criminal law and establishing civil liability."

Articles in the Declaration declare or stipulate, *inter alia*: any act of enforced disappearance is an offence to human dignity and places the persons concerned outside the protection of the law; no state shall practice, permit or tolerate enforced disappearances, and every state shall take effective necessary measures to prevent and terminate acts of disappearance; all acts of enforced disappearance shall be offences under criminal law and the state and its authorities and agents are liable under civil law for any acts of disappearance; there is no basis on which acts of enforced disappearance may be justified; states may not expel or forcibly return anyone to another state where there are substantial grounds to believe there exists the danger of enforced disappearance; the state must ensure the right to prompt and effective judicial remedy as a means to determine the whereabouts or state of health of persons deprived of liberty and/or identify the authority responsible for the detention or arrest; a person detained or arrested must be held in an officially recognized place of detention and the state must establish rules indicating which officials may order deprivation of liberty; a state must investigate all allegations of enforced disappearance and, when warranted, ensure that the person or persons responsible are held accountable before civil authorities; an act constituting enforced disappearance shall be considered a continuing offence as long as the fate and whereabouts of the disappeared person(s) remain unclarified; persons who have or are alleged to have committed acts of enforced disappearance shall not benefit from any special amnesty law or similar measure; victims of disappearance and their families shall have the right to redress and adequate compensation; states shall prevent and suppress the abduction of children of parents who have disappeared and of children born during the mother's enforced disappearance; and states must establish a process of review and annulment of cases of adoption of children of disappeared persons and children born during the mother's disappearance, but provide that such adoptions may continue if consent is given by a child's closest relatives.

The 1997 report of the WG states that progress in states' compliance with the Declaration has been extremely slow and that very few countries have enacted special legislation to make the act of enforced disappearance a specific offence under criminal law or to implement other provisions of the Declaration. The WG has taken up the practice, with the aims of making the Declaration better known and drawing the attention of governments to their responsibilities, of adopting general comments on specific provisions of the Declaration.

The 1997 report of the Working Group notes that more than 43,000 cases, related to the period between 1980 and 1996, remain under active consideration. In some instances, the cases relate to past situations of intense internal armed conflict or military dictatorships. In others, the numbers reflect armed conflict that may be either internal or transborder or have elements of both. Commentary in the report shows that individuals working in some professions are more vulnerable than others but that, in general, all sectors of society are potential targets. For example, victims have included journalists, medical doctors, university professors, students, civil servants, farmers, tourists, members of opposition political parties, members of groups in armed opposition, human rights advocates, lawyers, members of ethnic groups, civilians in territories under dispute, religious leaders, relatives of missing or disappeared persons and members of civic human rights groups and non-governmental organizations.

At its 1997 session, the Commission adopted a resolution by consensus (1997/26) related to disappearances and the mandate of the WG. The Commission, *inter alia*: expressed concern at the intensification of disappearances in various regions and the growing number of reports of harassment, ill-treatment and intimidation of witnesses and relatives of disappeared persons; reminded the WG that its primary role is to act as a channel of communication between families of disappeared persons and governments; reminded the WG of its humanitarian task and the need for it to observe UN standards and practices related to the handling of communications and consideration of government replies; reminded the WG that it should continue to consider the question of impunity, giving due regard to relevant provisions in the Declaration; reminded the WG to give particular attention to cases of disappeared children and children of disappeared persons; reminded the WG to apply a gender perspective in the reporting process, including in information collection and formulation of recommendations; deplored the failure of some governments to provide substantive replies on cases referred to them; urged governments to cooperate fully with the WG, to protect families of disappeared persons, and to invite the Group to make an in-country visit; urged governments with unresolved cases arising from previous practices and regimes to continue efforts to clarify outstanding cases; reminded governments of the need to conduct impartial inquiries, within a reasonable time period, into all alleged cases of disappearance; reminded governments of their duty to prosecute perpetrators of disappearances; invited states to take legislative, administrative, legal and other steps to implement the Declaration; noted the activities of NGO's in support of implementation of the Declaration; and, requested the Secretary-General to take further steps to ensure wide dissemination of the Declaration.

Renewal of the mandate of the Working Group for a further three years will be decided at the 1998 session of the Commission.

**\* \* \* \* \* \* \* \***

# ECONOMIC, SOCIAL AND CULTURAL RIGHTS

**Open-Ended Working Group on structural adjustment programmes:** (E/CN.4/1997/20)

At its 1996 session, the Commission decided to establish an open-ended Working Group (WG) with a mandate to elaborate policy guidelines on structural adjustment programmes (Decision 1996,103). The WG met for one week prior to the 1997 session of the Commission. In addition to representatives of 27 governments, those who attended included representatives of the International Labour Organization, the International Monetary Fund, the World Bank, and nine non-governmental organizations.

The report of the meeting identified key considerations in the IMF/World Bank approach to structural adjustment which included, *inter alia*: a firm anti-inflationary monetary policy; a sustainable fiscal strategy; a realistic exchange rate; appropriate structural policies that provide a market-friendly environment for growth; a development strategy focussed on growth and suited to a country's resources and needs; a liberal trade and exchange regime that fosters international trade and investment; sound and active social policies, including well-targeted social safety nets to alleviate poverty and protect the most vulnerable from any short-term negative impact of adjustment and reform; policies that promote greater equality of opportunity; and good governance-related to the need for publicly accountable government, participatory government and transparent legal and regulatory frameworks that are fair and limited to what is strictly necessary.

Acknowledging that the central goal of the World Bank is the eradication of poverty, the report summarized questions that arose, including those related to: the need for balance between the right to development and structural adjustment programmes; the impact of conditionalities on national sovereignty and the ability of states to make independent policy decisions; the conflict of interest between government constituencies, composed of electors, and the World Bank, composed of shareholders; the impact of debt servicing on available resources for education and other social services;

the impact of cuts in social spending and labour market flexibility on access to jobs; excessive interest rates; the growing imbalance between private and public investment; future World Bank policies to channel international financial flows from speculation to social development; the conflict between World Bank understanding of good governance (e.g., advocacy of judicial reforms aimed at privatization and free markets) and concerns of human rights bodies aimed at protecting human rights; the World Bank approach to poverty alleviation; and use of social indicators.

Annex I of the WG's report contains principles and policy guidelines, some of which were discussed at the meeting and some of which were presented for future discussion. Among the principles raised were that: it is the responsibility of all states to promote economic, social and cultural development; every government has the primary role and ultimate responsibility of ensuring the social progress and well-being of its people; all human rights and fundamental freedoms are indivisible, interdependent and should receive equal attention; the human person is the central subject of development and should be the active participant and beneficiary of the right to development; structural adjustment programmes should contribute to modernization, diversification and growth of economies in developing countries, while aimed at improving the standard of living, quality of life, health, education and employment of all people; negotiations between governments and international financial institutions (IFIs) on structural adjustment programmes should include consideration of human rights dimensions and aspects; the IFIs should adopt a more flexible approach in negotiations on borrowing conditions to take into account social indicators at both the national and regional levels; regarding privatization, emphasis should be given to creation of a private sector; structural adjustment policies must be consistent with article 28 of the Universal Declaration, entitling everyone to a social and international order in which the rights and freedoms set out in the UDHR can be fully realized; the policies of the World Bank and IMF must be brought into line with international human rights standards; the World Bank and IMF must be democratized and made subject to monitoring and guidance by ECOSOC and the General Assembly; legislative and regulatory frameworks should be established to ensure effective participation of all elements of society through the development process; states should simplify administrative regulations, disseminate information about public policy issues and facilitate maximum access to information; states should ensure greater transparency in negotiations and agreements between themselves; states should adjust policies and programmes to promote a more equitable distribution of productive assets, wealth, opportunities, income and services; states should ensure equal access to services and resources in the areas of education, health, food, housing, employment and distribution of income; states should safeguard and promote respect for basic workers' rights, prohibit forced labour and child labour, ensure equal pay for work of equal value and non-discrimination in employment; and states should promote reforms aimed at elimination of discrimination and exploitation and achievement of high rates of growth and social progress.

The annex to the report also contained commentary on conditionality, external pressure or intervention in the internal or external affairs of a state, availability of external resources, foreign debt, external trade, transnational corporations, development assistance, and international institutions, the latter including international non-governmental organizations.

The report recommended that the Commission authorize the WG to meet again for one week prior to the CHR's 1998 session and be mandated to gather and analyse information on the effects of structural adjustment programmes on the realization of economic, social and cultural rights and elaborate basic policy guidelines to serve as a basis for continued dialogue between human rights bodies and the IFIs. The report also requested the Commission, *inter alia*, to appoint an independent expert (an economist with expertise in the area of structural adjustment programmes) to: 1) undertake a study on the effects of structural adjustment policies on economic, social and cultural rights; 2) update previous work done on the subject within the UN; and 3) submit a consolidated study and draft set of guidelines to the 1998 session of the Commission.

At the 1997 session, the Commission adopted a resolution by roll call vote (1997/103) in response to the WG's report in which the CHR, *inter alia*: noted the report of the open-ended WG; authorized the Group to meet for one week, at least four weeks in advance of the 1998 session; assigned to the WG the mandate to gather and analyse information on the effects of structural adjustment on economic, social and cultural rights, elaborate basic policy guidelines to serve as a basis for continued dialogue between human rights bodies and international financial institutions and report to 1998 session of Commission; appointed an independent expert to study the effects of structural adjustment policies on economic, social and cultural rights, update previous work done on this subject within and outside the UN and submit a consolidated study, including a draft set of guidelines, to the 1998 session; requested the Secretary-General to circulate the study to all governments, UN bodies, regional commissions and non-governmental entities and invite them to submit comments to the next session of WG; and, requested the Secretary-General to invite and encourage NGOs involved in development and working in the field to participate in the sessions of the WG.

The vote on the resolution was 36 in favour and 13 opposed, with 3 abstentions. Renewal of the mandate of the Working Group is taken on an annual basis.

***\* \* \* \* \* \* \* \****

# EVICTIONS

**General Comment No. 7 (1997) of the Committee on Economic, Social and Cultural Rights** (E/C.12/1997/4) on the right to housing (art. 11.1 of the Covenant): forced evictions

The Committee defines "forced evictions" as the permanent or temporary removal against their will of individuals, families and/or communities from the homes and/or land which they occupy, without the provision of, and access to, appropriate forms of legal or other protection. The Committee notes that the practice of forced evictions is widespread and affects persons in both developed and developing countries, and that forced evictions frequently violate other human rights. While forced evictions might appear to occur primarily in heavily populated urban areas, it also takes place in

connection with forced population transfers, internal displacement, forced relocations in the context of armed conflict, mass exodus, and refugee movements; further that many forced evictions are associated with violence, while other instances occur in the name of development.

The Committee notes, *inter alia,* that: the obligations of States Parties to the Covenant in relation to forced evictions are based on article 11.1, read in conjunction with other relevant provisions, especially article 2.1, which obliges states to use "all appropriate means" to promote the right to adequate housing; the state itself must refrain from forced evictions and ensure that the law is enforced against its agents or third parties; the state's obligation to ensure respect for that right is not qualified by considerations related to its available resources; legislation against forced evictions is an essential basis upon which to build a system of effective protection; women, children, youth, older persons, indigenous people, ethnic and other minorities, and other vulnerable individuals and groups all suffer disproportionately from the practice of forced eviction; women in all groups are especially vulnerable given the extent of statutory and other forms of discrimination which often apply in relation to property rights (including home ownership) or rights of access to property or accommodation, and their particular vulnerability to acts of violence and sexual abuse when rendered homeless; forced eviction and housing demolition as a punitive measure are inconsistent with the norms of the Covenant; State Parties shall ensure, prior to carrying out any evictions, that all feasible alternatives are explored in consultation with the affected persons; legal remedies and procedures must be provided to those who are affected by the eviction orders; individuals concerned have a right to adequate compensation for any property, both personal and real, which is affected; in cases where eviction is considered to be justified, it should be carried out in strict compliance with relevant provisions of international human rights law and in accordance with general principles of reasonableness and proportionality; evictions should not result in individuals being rendered homeless or vulnerable to the violation of other rights; international agencies should scrupulously avoid involvement in development projects which involve large-scale evictions or displacement of persons without the provision of all appropriate protection and compensation; and, where institutions such as the World Bank have adopted guidelines on relocation and/or resettlement, with a view to limiting the scale of and human suffering associated with force evictions, there should be full respect for such guidelines insofar as they reflect the obligations contained in the Covenant.

**Comprehensive Human Rights Guidelines on Development-based Displacement** (E/CN.4/Sub.2/1997/7)

Less than a month after the adoption of General Comment No. 7, the UN Centre for Human Rights convened an Expert Seminar on Forced Evictions (Geneva, 11 to 15 June 1997) with a view to developing a set of comprehensive guidelines on development-based displacement. The mandate for the meeting originated with the Sub-Commission. The Guidelines were drafted by seven independent experts from the Dominican Republic, Kenya, Mexico, Netherlands, Pakistan, Philippines and South Africa, who took into account submissions and interventions by representatives of various governments, UN agencies, and NGOs.

The experts recognized the widespread nature of the practice of forced evictions and that, when forced evictions are carried out, they can occur in a variety of contexts including, but not limited to: conflicts over land rights, development and infrastructure projects; land acquisition measures associated with urban renewal; housing renovation; city beautification programmes; the clearing of land for agricultural purposes or macro-urban projects; unbridled speculation in land; and the holding of major international events such as the Olympic Games. Conscious of the fact that forced evictions intensify social conflict and inequality and invariably affect the poorest, most socially and economically vulnerable sectors of society, specifically women, children and indigenous people, the expert group resolved to protect human rights and prevent violations due to the practice of forced evictions, by adopting, *inter alia,* the following guidelines:

▶ While responsibility for forced evictions under international law is ultimately held by states, other entities -in particular, occupying powers, international financial and other institutions or organizations, transnational corporations and individual third parties, including public and private landlords or landowners-are not relieved from obligations in this regard.

▶ States should apply appropriate civil or criminal penalties against any person or entity, within their jurisdiction, carrying out any forced evictions not in full conformity with applicable law and these Guidelines.

▶ States should object, through the appropriate international legal mechanisms, to the carrying out of such forced evictions in other states;

▶ States should ensure that international organizations in which they are represented refrain from sponsoring or implementing any project, programme or policy which may involve such forced evictions.

▶ States have the obligation of maximum effective protection by: providing security of tenure against the practice of forced evictions for all persons under their jurisdiction, especially for indigenous peoples, women and children, female-headed households and persons belonging to vulnerable groups; ensuring that adequate and effective legal or other appropriate remedies are available to any persons whose protection against forced evictions has been violated or is under threat; and that impact assessments are carried out prior to the initiation of any project which could result in development-based displacement.

▶ States should ensure that no persons, groups or communities are rendered homeless or are exposed to the violation of any other human rights as a consequence of forced evictions.

▶ States should review relevant national legislation to ensure that its laws are compatible with the norms contained in these Guidelines and other relevant international human rights provisions, and states should adopt appropriate legislation and policies to ensure the protection of individuals, groups and communities from forced evictions.

▶ States should fully explore all possible alternatives to any act involving forced eviction; and, in this regard, all affected persons shall have the right to all relevant information and the right to full participation and consultation throughout the entire process and to propose any alternatives. If agreement cannot be reached on a proposed alternative, an independent body — such as a court of law, tribunal, or ombudsman — may be called upon.

▶ States should expropriate housing or land only as a last resort, unless its acquisition is to facilitate the enjoyment of human rights (for example, measures of land reform or redistribution), and in such cases, such action shall be (a) determined and envisaged by law and norms consistent with internationally recognized human rights; (b) solely for the purpose of protecting the general welfare in a democratic society; (c) reasonable and proportional; and (d) in accordance with the present Guidelines.

▶ All persons have the right to adequate housing which includes, *inter alia*, the integrity of the home, access to and protection of common property resources, and protection against any arbitrary or unlawful interference with privacy or respect of the home.

▶ All persons, irrespective of their tenure status, have a right of security of tenure which provides sufficient legal protection from forced eviction from one's home or land.

▶ All persons threatened with forced eviction have the right to: (a) a fair hearing before a competent, impartial and independent court or tribunal; (b) legal counsel and, where necessary, sufficient legal aid; and (c) effective remedies.

▶ All persons have a right to appeal any judicial or other decisions affecting their rights as established pursuant to the present Guidelines to the highest judicial authority.

▶ All persons subjected to any forced eviction not in full accordance with the present Guidelines should have a right to compensation for any losses of land or personal, real or other property or goods.

▶ All persons, groups and communities subjected to forced evictions have the right, but shall not be forced to return to their homes, lands or places of origin.

▶ In instances in which it is in the public interest, or where the safety, health or enjoyment of human rights so demands, particular persons and communities may be subject to resettlement; however, such resettlement must occur in a just and equitable manner and in full accordance with the law of general application.

▶ The right to resettlement includes the right to alternative land or housing which is safe, secure, accessible, affordable and habitable.

**Sub-Commission Resolution on Forced Evictions** (Resolution 1997/6)

At its 1997 session, the Sub-Commission adopted a resolution by consensus on the question of forced evictions. The resolution recalled the analytical report on forced evictions prepared by the Secretary-General in 1994 (E/CN.4/1994/20); reaffirmed that everyone has the right to a secure place to live in peace and dignity, which includes the right not to be evicted arbitrarily or on a discriminatory basis from one's home, land or community; noted that when, under exceptional circumstances, evictions are considered to be justified, such evictions must be carried out in strict compliance with relevant human rights provisions, and that such evictions must not result in individuals being rendered homeless or vulnerable to other human rights violations; emphasized that ultimate legal and political responsibility for preventing forced evictions rests with governments; noted the adoption of general comment No. 7 (1997) on forced evictions by the Committee on Economic, Social and Cultural Rights (E/C.12/1997/4); welcomed the report of the expert seminar on the practice of forced evictions and the comprehensive human rights guidelines adopted on development-based displacement (E/CN.4/Sub.2/1997/7); reaffirmed that forced evictions may often constitute gross violations of a broad range of rights, in particular, the right to adequate housing, the right to remain, the right to freedom of movement, the right to privacy, the right to property, the right to an adequate standard of living, the right to security of the home, the right to security of the person, the right to security of tenure, and the right to equality of treatment; strongly urged governments:

‣ to undertake immediately measures at all levels aimed at eliminating the practice of forced eviction by, *inter alia,* ensuring the right to security of tenure of all residents;

‣ to confer legal security of tenure on all persons, including all women and men who are currently threatened with forced eviction, and to adopt all necessary measures giving full protection against unreasonable eviction, based upon effective participation, consultation and negotiation with affected persons or groups; and

‣ to provide immediate restitution, compensation and/or appropriate and sufficient alternative accommodation of land, consistent with their rights and needs, to persons and communities that have been forcibly evicted.

\* \* \* \* \* \* \* \*

# EXECUTIONS AND THE DEATH PENALTY

## Special Rapporteur on extrajudicial, summary or arbitrary execution (E/CN.4/1997/60; E/CN.4/1997/ 60/Add.1)

The mandate of the Special Rapporteur (SR) was established by the Commission in 1982. In 1997, the SR was Mr. Bacré W. Ndiaye (Senegal). The mandate currently sets out the following tasks for the SR: continue to examine situations of extrajudicial, summary or arbitrary executions; respond effectively to information brought to the SR's attention; enhance further dialogue with governments; apply a gender perspective to the work; continue monitoring the implementation of international standards on safeguards and restrictions related to capital punishment; pay particular attention to extrajudicial, summary or arbitrary executions related to women and children; pay particular attention to violence against participants in demonstrations and other peaceful public manifestations; pay particular attention to violence against persons belonging to minorities; and pay particular attention to such executions where the victims are individuals carrying out peaceful activities in defence of human rights and fundamental freedoms.

The SR's 1997 report notes that action was taken on cases related to:

‣ imposition of the death penalty following unfair trials, or when the right of appeal or the right to seek pardon or commutation of sentence are denied, or in cases involving minors, mentally retarded or insane persons, pregnant women or recent mothers;

‣ death threats and fear of imminent extrajudicial/ summary/arbitrary execution by state officials, paramilitary groups, private individuals or groups cooperating with or tolerated by government, and unidentified persons who may be linked to one of the above;

‣ deaths in custody owing to torture, neglect, use of force or life-threatening conditions of detention;

‣ deaths from use of force, which exceeds the principles of necessity and proportionality, by law enforcement officials or persons acting in direct or indirect compliance with the state;

‣ deaths resulting from attacks by security forces, paramilitary groups, death squads or private forces operating with or tolerated by government;

‣ deaths during armed conflict, especially among the civilian population and non-combatants, contrary to international humanitarian law;

‣ expulsion, refoulement or return of persons to a country or place where their lives are in danger;

‣ genocide;

‣ breach of the obligation to investigate alleged violations of the right to life and to bring those responsible to justice; and

‣ breach of the obligation to provide adequate compensation to victims of violations of the right to life.

The report notes that between 25 November 1995 and 1 November 1996, the SR sent urgent appeals on behalf of more than 1,100 individuals, and allegations of executions on behalf of more than 1,300 other persons. The report notes that violations of the right to life have affected persons from many different professions and class or social status. Victims have included members of certain families, members of trade unions and human rights organizations, community workers, religious activists, writers and journalists, members of political parties, persons belonging to ethnic, linguistic or national minorities, members of rebel groups and civilians caught in areas affected by armed conflict.

In terms of the situation of women, the SR states that action was taken on behalf of more than 80 women. He points out that this figure reflects only those cases in which it was specifically indicated that the victim was female and does not necessarily show the actual number of women on whose behalf the SR intervened. The report notes that in some cases, sources do not indicate whether the victim is male or female and the gender cannot be determined by the name; in other cases, allegations refer to groups of unidentified civilians (e.g., the displaced population of a given region) without gender specification. The SR further states that the relatively low percentage of cases involving women may reflect the underrepresentation of women in the political and economic life of the country, thereby causing women to be perceived as less of a threat and therefore less exposed to acts of violence by governments. The report notes that, where women have been active in areas more traditionally occupied by men, they have been as vulnerable to threats, attacks and summary execution as men. As well, in a number of cases, women have been targeted because of their relationship to men who were persecuted by security forces.

In other sections, the report includes summary information on violations of the right to life related to children, mass exoduses, the right to freedom of opinion and expression, the administration of justice, persons belonging to national, ethnic, religious or linguistics minorities, terrorism, activities in defence of human rights, and reprisals against persons who have cooperated with representatives of UN human rights bodies.

On the question of the capital punishment, the report outlines the three principles that have guided the Special Rapporteur's work. These are:

▸ the desirability of the abolition of the death penalty-citing the Security Council resolutions establishing the international tribunals for the former Yugoslavia and Rwanda and the provision that imprisonment is the only penalty that may be imposed by these tribunals; the comment of the Human Rights Committee that, while states are not obliged to abolish the death penalty, they are required to limit its use to only the most serious crimes; General Assembly resolutions aimed at progressively restricting the number of offences for which capital punishment may be imposed; the report of the Secretary-General and the resolution of ECOSOC on the safeguards to protect the rights of those facing the death penalty;

▸ the need to ensure the highest standards of independence, competence, objectivity and impartiality of judges and juries and full respect of guarantees for a fair trial-related to the absolute need to ensure defendants in capital cases access to competent counsel, the presumption of innocence, due account being given to mitigating factors, requirements that the burden of proof rest with the state, provisions for review and appeal by a higher tribunal, the rights to seek pardon, commutation of sentence or clemency, special jurisdictions and the requirement for a public and transparent trial; and

▸ restrictions on the use of the death penalty-related to issues beyond the prohibition in international law on the application of the death penalty in cases involving juvenile offenders, mentally retarded or insane persons, pregnant women and recent mothers, and use of the death penalty for economic crimes and drug-related offences; ECOSOC resolution 1984/50 stating that the scope of crimes subject to the death penalty should not exceed intentional crimes with lethal or other extremely grave consequences.

Consistent with the approach taken in previous reports, the SR includes commentary on the question of impunity and states that impunity remains the principal cause for the perpetuation of violations of human rights, and particularly those of the right to life. The report notes conditions conducive to impunity, including: legislation that exempts perpetrators of human rights violations from prosecution; failure of authorities to invoke legal provisions for the prosecution of human

rights violators; failure of authorities to investigate allegations of human rights violations; absence of an independent and impartial judiciary; and use of military courts to try members of the security forces. The report also considers two other issues related to impunity: (a) mob killings in which suspected robbers, suspected murderers, members of discriminated groups and even persons responsible for traffic accidents are often summarily executed in the streets by angry mobs; (b) international jurisdiction, noting the need for the establishment of a permanent international criminal court with universal jurisdiction over mass violations of human rights and humanitarian law and the adoption of a convention, similar to the Convention against Torture, which would provide domestic courts with international jurisdiction over persons suspected of having committed mass violations of the right to life.

The recommendations included in the report are offered under the general recommendation that "The international community should concentrate its efforts on the effective prevention of further human rights crises, and on the implementation of existing standards for the protection of the right to life." Following on this, the report recommends that states:

▸ which have not done so ratify the International Covenant on Civil and Political Rights and, in particular, its Second Optional Protocol;

▸ bring national laws into conformity with international standards, particularly in regard to the prohibition on the imposition of the death sentence on minors and the mentally ill;

▸ which enforce capital punishment laws, observe all fair trial standards;

▸ establish a minimum period of six months following sentencing in capital cases to allow for appeal;

▸ investigate all instances brought to their attention of death threats or attempts against the lives of others;

▸ ensure that conditions of detention conform to international standards and law;

▸ ensure that security personnel receive training on restrictions on the use of force and firearms, including methods of crowd control without resorting to lethal force;

▸ which have not done so, ratify the four Geneva Conventions of 1949 and the two Additional Protocols;

▸ in which terrorists groups are active, conduct counter-insurgency operations in conformity with human rights standards;

▸ which have not done so, ratify the Convention on the Prevention and Punishment of the Crime of Genocide;

▸ take all necessary measures to prevent acts of communal violence from degenerating into large-scale killings that may reach the dimension of genocide;

▸ at all times, refrain from any propaganda or incitement to hatred and intolerance that might give rise to acts of communal violence or condone such acts;

▸ refrain from expelling persons in circumstances where respect for their right to life is not fully guaranteed;

- conduct exhaustive and impartial investigations into allegations of violations of the right to life, identify those responsible and prosecute alleged perpetrators of such acts;

- not resort to blanket amnesty laws prohibiting the prosecution of alleged perpetrators and violating the rights of the victims; and

- include in their national legislation provisions to allow adequate compensation and facilitate access to judicial remedies to victims and families of victims of violations of the right to life.

The report includes three other recommendations, namely that:

- the Commission on Human Rights consider appointing a special rapporteur on conditions of detention and prison conditions;

- the Commission call for rapid adoption of an optional protocol to the Convention against Torture to establish a system of periodic visits to places of detention; and

- a monitoring mechanism to supervise implementation of the Convention on the Prevention and Punishment of the Crime of Genocide be established.

The mandate of the Special Rapporteur is up for renewal at the Commission's 1998 session.

At its 1997 session, the Commission adopted by consensus a resolution (1997/61) related to the mandate of the SR. The Commission, *inter alia*: expressed alarm that extrajudicial, summary or arbitrary executions continue in all parts of the world on a large scale; expressed dismay at the practice of impunity and noted it as a main cause of continued occurrence of such executions; strongly condemned once again all the extrajudicial, summary or arbitrary executions that continue to take place throughout the world; demanded that governments ensure that the practice is eliminated; reiterated the obligation of governments to conduct impartial and exhaustive investigations into all suspected cases of such executions; encouraged states that have not abolished the death penalty to comply with obligations under relevant provisions of international human rights instruments; requested the SR to continue work and submit reports to the Commission annually and exceptionally if required; requested the SR to give particular attention to executions of children as well as participants in demonstrations and other peaceful public manifestations or persons belonging to minorities; requested the SR to give special attention to executions against persons carrying out peaceful activities in defence of human rights and fundamental freedoms; urged governments to take the necessary steps to prevent loss of life during public manifestations, internal and communal violence, disturbances, tension and public emergency or armed conflict; appealed to governments to ensure that all persons deprived of liberty are treated with humanity and respect; urged governments to cooperate with and assist the SR, including where appropriate by inviting the SR to conduct field missions; and, expressed concern at number of governments noted in the 1997 report that have not replied to communications from the SR.

**Resolution on the Death Penalty**

The Commission also adopted, by roll call vote, a resolution on the question of the death penalty (1997/12) in which the Commission, *inter alia*: recalled relevant articles in the International Covenant on Civil and Political Rights and the Convention on the Rights of the Child; welcomed the opening for signature of the Second Optional protocol to the ICCPR, aimed at abolition of the death penalty; recalled numerous ECOSOC resolutions on the subject; welcomed exclusion of capital punishment from penalties that may be imposed by the international criminal tribunals on the former Yugoslavia and Rwanda; expressed concern that several countries impose the death penalty in disregard to provisions in the ICCPR and the Convention on the Rights of the Child; expressed concern that several countries do not take into account the international Safeguards guaranteeing protection of the rights of those facing the death penalty; expressed belief that abolition of the death penalty contributes to enhancement of human dignity and progressive development of human rights; called on states parties to the ICCPR that have not yet done so to consider acceding to or ratifying the Second Optional Protocol; urged all states that maintain the death penalty to comply fully with obligations under the ICCPR and the Convention on the Rights of the Child and impose the death sentence only for the most serious crimes, not to persons under 18 years of age, exclude pregnant women and ensure the right to seek pardon or commutation; called on all states progressively to restrict the number of crimes for which the death sentence may be imposed; called on states that still impose the death penalty to consider suspending executions with a view to abolishing the death penalty; requests that the Secretary-General submit yearly a supplement to the quinquennial report on capital punishment and implementation of the Safeguards, on changes in law and practice concerning the death penalty worldwide; and, called on states that maintain the death penalty to make available to the public information regarding imposition of the death penalty.

\* \* \* \* \* \* \* \*

# FREEDOM OF OPINION AND EXPRESSION

**Special Rapporteur on freedom of opinion and expression** (E/CN.4/1997/31)

The mandate of the Special Rapporteur (SR) on freedom of opinion and expression was established by the Commission in 1993. In 1997, the SR was Mr. A. Hussain (India). In making this decision, the Commission explicitly acknowledged the cause-and-effect relationship between violations of the rights to opinion, expression and information and arbitrary detention, summary execution, disappearance, persecution and intimidation, harassment and other acts of violence and other forms of violations.

The 1997 report reviews some of the basic questions addressed in previous reports and taken by the SR as the framework within which the right must be viewed. Among the points made are: the principle of proportionality must be applied in establishing whether a limitation on the right is legitimate; protection of the right is the rule and restriction is the exception; the provisions of article 19 of the ICCPR, however, must be read in conjunction with those of article 20 related to the prohibition on propaganda for war and the advocacy of racial hatred; the tendency to perpetuate or concentrate excessive and arbitrary authority in the executive branch erodes freedom of opinion and expression and restricts the independence of the judiciary and legal system; any appeal on the part of the state to restrict freedom of opinion and expression should meet strict requirements indicating necessity; states should not invoke custom, tradition or religious considerations to restrict the right; states should review specific laws intended to protect national security as well as ordinary criminal laws which may be used to infringe, restrict or obliterate the right; the right to seek, receive and impart information is not simply a converse of the right to opinion and expression but a separate freedom; the right of everyone to receive information must be adequately protected and its protection must be the rule and not the exception; and the tendency of governments to withhold information from the people through measures such as censorship is to be strongly checked.

With these principles in mind, the SR addressed communications to governments related to, for example: actions against editors and journalists for publishing state secrets and publishing false information; deliberate killings of press professionals; closures of newspapers; assaults on journalists; actions against pro-democracy activists; arrests and trials of activists on charges of subversion; violent suppression of student demonstrations; arrests of members of opposition political parties; actions against elected members of national assemblies; and, restrictions on lawyers and persons working for human rights organizations. The section of the report dealing with conclusions and recommendations notes that violations of the rights to freedom of opinion and expression and to seek, receive and impart information often concur with violations of other human rights, including those related to disappearances, summary/arbitrary execution, torture, religious intolerance and arbitrary detention, as well as the problem of terrorism. In this regard, the SR stated that the right to freedom of expression can be described as an essential test right, the enjoyment of which illustrates the degree of enjoyment of all human rights. As well, he emphasized that actions by governments to ban certain publications, disband independent organizations and unions, and rescind or deny licences to independent media are frequently good indicators of situations in which the protection of all human rights will, in future, be weakened.

In the commentary on women's human rights, the SR called on states actively to support women attempting to make their voices heard and to ensure that they are welcomed as active participants in public life. Following on this, he urged governments to take effective measures to eliminate the atmosphere of fear that prevents many women from communicating freely on their own behalf or on behalf of other women who have been victims of violence, either in domestic or community settings, or as a result of internal or transborder conflict. The report also reflected on the need to establish, in cooperation with the SR on violence against women, a framework through which violations of women's right to freedom of expression can be systematically documented and addressed. In this regard, he urged organizations and associations working on women's human rights to establish closer links with NGOs for which freedom of opinion and expression is the primary mandate.

On the right to development, the SR underlined the link between the right of people, both individually and collectively, to participate in public life and the rights to freedom of opinion and expression and to seek, receive and impart information. The report stated that, as discussions on the implementation of the right to development continue, laws and governmental practices which violate the rights to freedom of opinion, expression, information, dissent, association and participation must be taken into account. The SR noted violations in this context, including suppression of political expression, denial of access to family planning information for women, discrimination against women through personal status laws, prohibition on the establishment of independent trade unions, prohibitions or restrictions on the operation of independent media, restrictions on access to information on subjects of public interest and importance, suppression of the use of minority languages, infringements on the right to freedom of conscience, belief and religion, restrictions on the right to peaceful assembly, repression of the right to peaceful dissent, and resort to arguments based on a supposed need to maintain discipline or political order and stability, or respond to the imperative of modernization and nation-building. The SR stated that the rights to freedom of opinion and expression and to seek and receive information are fundamental prerequisites to ensure public participation, without which the realization of the right to development, as a prerogative of people rather than states, will remain in jeopardy.

Renewal of the mandate on freedom of opinion and expression will be considered at the 1999 session of the Commission.

At its 1997 session, the Commission adopted a resolution by consensus (1997/27) related to the mandate in which it, *inter alia*: referred to the rights and duties set out in article 19 of the ICCPR; noted the bases on which the right may be restricted; noted the need to ensure that national security is not used unjustifiably to restrict the right; noted the Johannesburg Principles on National Security, Freedom of Expression and Access to Information; considered the rights to opinion, expression, information, peaceful assembly and association to be essential to popular participation in the decision-making process; considered the possibility that a deterioration in the protection of the right could indicate a weakening in the protection and enjoyment of other rights; reaffirmed the interrelationship and interdependence of the right to opinion and expression and the right to seek, receive and impart information; reaffirmed that education is an integral component of effective participation in a free society and that the eradication of illiteracy is important; expressed concern at the numerous reports of detention, discrimination, acts of violence, harassment, persecution and intimidation against professionals in the field of information; noted the need to raise awareness about the interrelationship between the use and availability of new media of communication, including modern telecommunications technology, and the rights to expression and information; expressed concern at the gap for women between the existence of the right and the actual enjoyment of the right; expressed concern at the extensive occurrence of detention, long-term detention, extrajudicial killing, persecution and harassment, abuse of legal provisions on criminal libel, threats, acts of violence and discrimination directed at persons, including professionals in the field of information, exercising or seeking to exercise the right to freedom of opinion and expression and the rights to freedom of thought, conscience and religion, peaceful assembly and association and the right to take part in the conduct of public affairs; expressed concern at state practices such as abuse of states of emergency and vague definitions of offences against state security; welcomed the release of persons formerly detained for exercising these rights and freedoms; appealed to states to ensure that persons exercising or seeking to exercise these rights do not suffer discrimination in areas such as employment, housing and social services; invited UN bodies, mechanisms and procedures to examine violations of the rights to expression and opinion from a gender perspective; invited the SR, in cooperation with the SR on violence against women, to pay particular attention to the relationship between the effective promotion and protection of the right to freedom of opinion and expression and incidents of discrimination based on sex, and consider how these obstacles impede the ability of women to make informed choices in areas of particular importance to them as well as in areas related to the general decision-making processes in the societies in which they live; invited the SR to develop further the commentary on the right to seek and receive information; invited the SR, in his report to the 1998 Commission, to consider all aspects of the impact of new information technology on equal opportunity of access to information and exercise of the right to expression as set out in the ICCPR; requested the SR to submit a report to the 1998 session

## \* \* \* \* \* \* \* \*
# HIV/AIDS AND HUMAN RIGHTS

At its 53rd session, the Commission on Human Rights (CHR) considered a report from the Secretary-General (E/CN.4/1997/37) on the Second International Consultation on HIV/AIDS and Human Rights which took place in Geneva, from 23 to 25 September 1996. A major outcome of the consultation was a set of Guidelines recommended by the expert participants for states on the promotion and protection of fundamental rights and freedoms in the context of HIV/AIDS, as well as strategies for their dissemination and implementation. The CHR adopted a resolution (1997/33) in which it: invited all states to consider these Guidelines; called upon the UN High Commissioner for Human Rights, the Joint UN Programme on HIV/AIDS (UNAIDS), its co-sponsors and other partners, to provide technical cooperation to states, upon request of governments when required, from within existing resources, for the promotion and protection of human rights in the context of HIV/AIDS; and requested the Secretary-General to solicit the opinion of governments, specialized agencies and international and non-governmental organizations and to prepare for consideration by the Commission at its 55th session (1999) a progress report on the follow-up to the present resolution.

The Sub-Commission, at its 1997 session, adopted a similar resolution (1997/40) welcoming the guidelines; calling on special rapporteurs, representatives and working groups, as well as other UN human rights bodies, to continue to incorporate HIV/AIDS-related issues, as appropriate, in all their

activities; and urging the CHR to keep the issue of HIV/AIDS-related human rights violations and discrimination under review.

## \* \* \* \* \* \* \* \*
# INDEPENDENCE OF JUDGES AND LAWYERS

**Special Rapporteur on the Independence of judges and lawyers** (E/CN.4/1997/32)

The mandate of the Special Rapporteur (SR) on the independence of judges and lawyers was established in 1994 and renewed for a further three years by the Commission at its 1997 session. In 1997, the SR was Mr. Param Cumaraswamy (Malaysia). The elements in the mandate include: investigation into allegations of interference in the judicial process; establishing a record of attacks against judges, lawyers and court officers; cataloguing the positive measures taken by governments to protect judges and lawyers and their independence; and making proposals on how to enhance the independence of judges of lawyers.

The 1997 report contains brief commentary on issues and cases related to, *inter alia*: removal of immunity from high court officials; threats and intimidation against and detention, abduction and killing of lawyers; a proposal to set up a separate regulatory body to licence lawyers to practice; disregard of court decisions by governments; dismissal of judges and magistrates from cases; proposed legislation that would infringe on the separation of powers; actions by military personnel in contravention of judicial orders; and, executive intimidation of judges — such as statements in favour of resignation and impeachment — whose rulings have offended or run counter to the wishes of the executive branch.

Other issues covered briefly in the report include: development of a mechanism to resolve disputes between the legal profession and the judiciary; establishment of an international criminal court-including provision for judges to be full-time members of the court with fixed remuneration to ensure the individual independence of members and the right for the prosecutor to initiate investigations rather than, as currently envisaged in the draft statute, limiting the right to launch investigations to cases initiated by states parties; the relationship between media and the judiciary, particularly in such areas as pre-trial publicity and its effects on the right to fair trial; and trial observation either by the Special Rapporteur (SR) or a person so designated.

The renewal of the mandate on the independence of judges and lawyers will be considered by the Commission at its session in the year 2000.

At its 1997 session, the Commission adopted a resolution by consensus (1997/23) referring to the work undertaken by the SR. The Commission, *inter alia*: affirmed that an independent and impartial judiciary and legal profession are essential prerequisites for protection of human rights and ensuring that there is no discrimination in the administration of justice; referred to the UN Basic Principles on the Independence of the Judiciary, the Basic Principles on the Role of Lawyers and the Guidelines on the Role of Prosecutors; noted with concern increasingly frequent attacks on the independence of judges, lawyers and court officers; invited the High Commissioner for Human Rights to collaborate with the SR on the elaboration of a manual on the training of judges and lawyers in the field of human rights; encouraged governments to invite the SR to conduct in-country visits; and, extended the mandate of the SR for a further three years.

**\* \* \* \* \* \* \* \***

# INDIGENOUS ISSUES

Issues of concern to indigenous peoples were addressed by both the Commission on Human Rights and the SubCommission on the Prevention of Discrimination and Protection of Minorities.

### Commission on Human Rights

The 1997 session of the Commission considered three reports relevant to indigenous peoples: (1) a report of the Secretary-General on the question of a permanent UN forum for indigenous peoples (E/CN.4/1997/100); (2) a report of the High Commissioner for Human Rights and the Coordinator for the International Decade of the World's Indigenous People (E/CN.4/1997/101); and, (3) a report by the Working Group on indigenous issues, related to a draft declaration on the rights of indigenous peoples (E/CN.4/ 1997/102). The Commission, by consensus, then adopted three resolutions and two draft decisions related to indigenous issues.

### Resolution on the Working Group to elaborate a draft declaration on the rights of indigenous peoples

In the first resolution, on the Working Group (WG) of the Commission to elaborate a draft declaration (1997/31), the Commission, *inter alia*: recalled the 1994 General Assembly decision to consider a draft declaration with the participation of representatives of indigenous peoples; welcomed the progress made in the elaboration of a text; emphasized the important and special nature of the draft declaration as an instrument specifically for promoting the rights of indigenous peoples; welcomed the continuation and positive nature of the deliberations of the WG elaborating the text; welcomed ECOSOC's decision to approve the participation of organizations of indigenous peoples in the process; urged ECOSOC to approve all pending applications for participation from such groups as soon as possible; recommended that the WG meet for 10 working days prior to the 1998 session of Commission; encouraged indigenous organizations not already involved in the process but wishing to be so to apply for authorization; and, requested the WG to report to the 1998 session.

### Resolution on the question of a permanent UN forum for indigenous peoples

The second resolution, on the question of a permanent forum (1997/30), *inter alia*: recalled the recommendation in the Vienna Declaration and Programme of Action that a permanent forum for indigenous peoples be considered; recalled General Assembly resolution 50/157 recognizing that consideration of establishing a permanent forum is one of the important objectives of the International Decade of the World's Indigenous People; noted the recommendation of the General Assembly that a second workshop on the possible establishment of a forum be considered; requested the High Commissioner for Human Rights to convene a second

workshop prior to the 1997 session of the Working Group on Indigenous Populations; requested the High Commissioner for Human Rights to transmit the report of the workshop to the Working Group and invite the Group to express its views; requested the High Commissioner to submit the report, with comments arising from discussions of the Working Group, to the 1998 CHR session as well as to governments, relevant UN bodies and indigenous organizations for comment and to submit these comments to the 1998 session.

### Resolution on the Working Group on indigenous populations and the International Decade of the World's Indigenous People

The third resolution (1997/32) *inter alia*: noted that international standards must be developed on the basis of the diverse situations and aspirations of the world's indigenous peoples; affirmed recognition of the value and diversity of the cultures and forms of social organization of indigenous peoples; affirmed that development of indigenous peoples within their countries will contribute to socio-economic, cultural and environmental advancement of all countries of the world; recalled the goal of the International Decade to strengthen international cooperation for a solution to problems faced by indigenous peoples in areas such as human rights, environment, development, education and health.

**I. Report of Working Group (WG):** urged the WG to continue the comprehensive review of developments and the diverse situations and aspirations of the world's indigenous peoples; invited the WG to take into account the work of thematic rapporteurs, representatives, experts and working groups, and expert seminars as it pertains to the situation of indigenous peoples; invited the WG to continue consideration as to whether there are ways in which the contribution of expertise from indigenous peoples to the work of the Group might be enhanced; encouraged all initiatives by governments, indigenous organizations and NGOs to ensure full participation of indigenous peoples in activities related to the tasks of the WG; appealed to governments, organizations and individuals to consider contributing to the Voluntary Fund for Indigenous Populations.

**II. International Decade:** welcomed the affirmation by General Assembly that a major objective of the Decade is the adoption of a declaration on the rights of indigenous peoples and another important objective is consideration of the establishment of a permanent forum; recommended that the High Commissioner for Human Rights assume responsibility for coordination of the Decade; requested the High Commissioner to consider organizing a workshop for research and higher education institutions focussing on indigenous issues in education, with the aim of improving the exchange of information between such institutions and encouraging further cooperation in future; requested the High Commissioner to submit to the 1998 CHR session an updated report on activities related to the Decade; encouraged governments to support the Decade by establishing national committees or other mechanisms involving indigenous peoples to ensure that the objectives and activities of the Decade are well planned and implemented on the basis of full partnership with indigenous peoples; encouraged governments to seek the means to give indigenous peoples greater responsibility for their own affairs and effective voice on matters which affect them; encouraged governments to identify resources for activities designed to implement the goals of the Decade; recommended that the High Commissioner, within the context of the Decade, give due regard to the development of human rights training for indigenous peoples; and, invited relevant UN institutions, programs and agencies to give increased priority and resources to improving the conditions of indigenous peoples, with particular emphasis on the needs of these peoples in developing countries.

### Decision related to the study on indigenous land rights

The fourth text, a draft decision, related to the study on indigenous land rights (1997/114) in which the Commission, *inter alia*: approved the appointment of a Special Rapporteur of the Sub-Commission to prepare a working paper on indigenous peoples and their relationship to land, with a view to suggesting practical measures to address ongoing problems in this regard; requested the Special Rapporteur to submit a preliminary working paper to the Working Group on Indigenous Populations and to transmit the paper to governments and indigenous organizations for views that should be taken into account in the preparation of a final paper to be submitted to the Working Group and the Sub-Commission at their 1998 sessions.

### Decision related to the study on treaties and other arrangements

The fifth text was also a draft decision (1997/113). In it, the Commission endorsed the decision of the Sub-Commission to request its Special Rapporteur (SR) to prepare a study on treaties, agreements and other constructive arrangements between states and indigenous populations and requested the SR to submit his final report to the 1997 sessions of the Working Group and the Sub-Commission.

### Sub-Commission on Prevention of Discrimination and Protection of Minorities

The Sub-Commission Working Group (WG) on Indigenous Populations was established in 1982 with a mandate to review developments related to the promotion and protection of human rights and fundamental freedoms of indigenous peoples and the evolution of standards concerning the rights of indigenous peoples, taking account of both the similarities and differences in the situations and aspirations of indigenous peoples throughout the world. The WG meets annually just prior to the session of the Sub-Commission. In 1994, the Commission requested that the WG take up the issue of the establishment of a permanent forum for indigenous people in the UN system, a subject which remains under consultation and discussion.

The conclusions and recommendations in the WG's report of its July/August 1997 meeting (E/CN.4/Sub.2/1997/ 14), *inter alia*: reaffirmed that the agenda item on standard-setting constituted a fundamental part of its mandate; noted the general consensus among the participants that a definition of "indigenous peoples" at the global level was not possible at this time, and certainly not necessary for the adoption of the draft UN declaration on the rights of indigenous peoples; addressed guidelines or codes of conduct for private sector energy and mining concerns and decided to include the question on the agenda of its next meeting; noted that there

continues to be serious problems for indigenous peoples related to environment, land and sustainable development; decided to highlight the issue of "indigenous peoples: education and language" at its next session; endorsed the recommendation of a workshop (on the establishment of a permanent forum), that the Commission on Human Rights at its 1998 session consider how to further the process towards the establishment of a permanent forum for indigenous people in the UN, in part through the drafting of concrete proposals and by considering the possibility of submitting the matter to ECOSOC for action; decided to focus, at its next session, on the questions of the membership, participation in and mandate of a possible permanent forum, including issues such as equitable geographical distribution on the basis of where indigenous peoples live and the open and authentic representation of indigenous nations, peoples, organizations and communities; and, welcomed the establishment by indigenous peoples of a committee on indigenous health issues for future cooperation with the Office of the High Commissioner for Human Rights, the Working Group and the World Health Organization (WHO).

At its August 1997 session, the Sub-Commission considered a number of issues related to indigenous peoples, only some of which were the subject of reports. These included:

(a) **The UN Voluntary Fund for Indigenous Populations**, which was established in 1985 to assist representatives of indigenous communities and organizations to participate in the deliberations of the Working Group on Indigenous Populations;

(b) **The International Decade of the World's Indigenous People,** which was proclaimed by the General Assembly in December 1993; the High Commissioner for Human Rights is now responsible for coordinating the activities of the Decade;

(c) **Religious freedom of indigenous peoples:** at its 1996 session, the Commission on Human Rights requested the CHR Special Rapporteur on religious intolerance to take into account in the work and field missions the specific problems faced by indigenous peoples related to the destruction and violation of their sacred sites and religious ceremonies. The Commission also invited the SR to take into account the spiritual relationship indigenous communities have with the land and the significance of traditional lands for the practice of their religion and to examine the history of events that have been responsible for the violation of freedom of religion and religious practice for these communities.

(d) **Special Rapporteur on the protection of the heritage of indigenous people:** based on working papers developed at the Sub-Commission in 1990 and 1991, the Commission decided in 1992 to appoint a Sub-Commission Special Rapporteur (SR) on the protection of the heritage of indigenous people. The SR was mandated to: undertake a comprehensive analysis of the laws and traditions of indigenous peoples with respect to the definition, ownership and control of cultural property; consider the relationship between indigenous cultural and intellectual property; and elaborate draft principles and guidelines for the protection of the heritage of indigenous peoples. The mandate of the SR was continued in 1997 to facilitate cooperation, coordination and the promotion of the full participation of indigenous peoples in work related to the protection of their heritage. Following a request by the Sub-Commission, a technical meeting was held in March 1997, attended by representatives of the World Intellectual Property Organization (WIPO), the United Nations Educational, Scientific and Cultural Organization (UNESCO), the United Nations Environmental Programme (UNEP), the United Nations Development Programme (UNDP), the Food and Agricultural Organization (FAO) and the World Trade Organization (WTO). The purpose of the meeting was to consider how these agencies could contribute to the work of the SR. The report of the technical meeting (E/CN.4/Sub.2/1997/15) included summary comments on discussions of the draft principles and guidelines elaborated by the SR and noted the importance of, for example: informed consent and the negotiating environment; fact-finding investigations; the protection against the destruction of indigenous cultures through, *inter alia*, ethnocide or cultural genocide; and, remuneration rights and control by indigenous peoples over their own knowledge.

(e) **Special Rapporteur on indigenous land rights:** In 1997, on the recommendation of the Sub-Commission, the Commission appointed a Special Rapporteur of the Sub-Commission to conduct a comprehensive study on the problem of recognition of and respect for indigenous land rights. The study was intended to include: (a) a detailed and updated account of the status of efforts to secure indigenous land rights and the problems that continue in that area; and (b) a catalogue of existing national laws, policies and procedures concerning indigenous land rights. The preliminary working paper on this subject was submitted to the 1997 Sub-Commission (E/CN.4/Sub.2/ 1997/17) and included commentary on: the relationship of indigenous peoples to their lands, territories and resources; history and background-the impact of the doctrines of dispossession; a framework for the analysis of contemporary problems regarding indigenous land rights; and, efforts to resolve indigenous land issues.

(f) **Special Rapporteur on treaties:** In 1989, the Commission confirmed the appointment of a Sub-Commission Special Rapporteur (SR) to undertake a study on treaties, agreements and other constructive arrangements between states and indigenous populations. The final report of the SR was not issued for or considered at the 1997 Sub-Commission and remains pending.

**Resolutions of the Sub-Commission:**

At its 1997 session, the Sub-Commission adopted resolutions on: a permanent forum for indigenous peoples (1997/10); the study on indigenous land rights (1997/12); protection of the heritage of indigenous peoples (1997/13); the Working Group on Indigenous Populations (1997/14); and the International Decade of the World's Indigenous People (1997/15). The Sub-Commission transmitted for action by the 1998 Commission, draft decisions on the permanent forum, the protection of the heritage of indigenous peoples and the Working Group on Indigenous Populations.

* * * * * * * *

# INTERNALLY DISPLACED PERSONS

**Representative of the Secretary-General on internally displaced persons** (E/CN.4/1997/43)

The mandate of the Representative of the Secretary-General on internally displaced persons was established in 1992. In 1997, the Representative was Mr. Francis Deng (Sudan). The emphasis in the mandate was to establish a better understanding of the general problems faced by internally displaced persons and their possible long-term solutions including, where required, recommendations on the ways and means of improving protection for and assistance to internally displaced persons. The work has evolved since that time and, in 1996, the three main areas of activity for the Representative were: development of appropriate legal standards for meeting the needs of the internally displaced; promoting the most effective international institutions to meet the challenges of protection; and, assisting the internally displaced and undertaking visits to countries with serious displacement problems to examine them on the ground. Corresponding responses to these three areas have been defined as being: the development of measures for pre-empting and preventing displacement; provision of adequate means of protection and relief assistance during displacement; and, establishment of durable solutions through voluntary and safe return, resettlement, rehabilitation, reconstruction, and self-reliant development.

At the 1997 session of the Commission, work on the situation of internally displaced persons was considered to include five elements:

‣ development of country profiles-to assist in the understanding of generic problems of displacement and create a dialogue with authorities on specific problems in the country concerned;

‣ development of a system for the collection of information on the problems of internal displacement around the world;

‣ assessment and evaluation of existing international law to determine the degree to which it provides an adequate basis for the protection of internally displaced persons and the development of an appropriate framework to ensure adequate protection;

‣ review and evaluation of existing international institutions, their mandates and operations, to determine the extent to which they provide protection for internally displaced persons; and

‣ development of a global strategy to enable the international community to respond coherently to the problem of internal displacement.

The report to the 1997 Commission builds on work in previous years and reviews key aspects in the normative framework through which protection of the rights of internally displaced persons is either guaranteed or not. Commentary on this subject covered a number of key points including that:

‣ gaps in international protection arise in certain areas such as those related to personal documentation or restitution or compensation for property lost during displacement;

▶ existing provisions of human rights law are limited in their application to specific situations, such as armed conflict, or to categories of persons such as children, refugees or minorities;

▶ a general norm for protection may exist but a more specific right may not be provided — e.g., freedom of movement but no explicit right to find refuge in a safe area or not to be forcibly returned to places of danger;

▶ in situations of tension, but falling short of armed conflict, humanitarian law does not apply and human rights law may be restricted or derogated from; and

▶ human rights law binds only states and not non-state actors such as insurgent groups in whose territory internally displaced persons may be located.

The report noted that these and other considerations relate to the rights and protections of people once they are displaced and that a second study, as a companion to the one on the normative framework, was under way on the content and limitations of a right not to be displaced. It is anticipated that the findings of these two studies will provide the basis for the development of guiding principles applicable before displacement occurs, those that apply in actual situations of internal displacement, and those that apply to the post-displacement phase.

The report considers in some detail elements in the existing institutional framework and points out:

▶ at present, there is no institution with exclusive responsibility for the internally displaced;

▶ it is the view of many that there should not be one institution mandated to assume this responsibility because, in part, the problem of internal displacement exceeds the capacities of any single organization;

▶ an effective framework for dealing with internal displacement requires bringing together the humanitarian, human rights and development regimes into a comprehensive approach;

▶ existing capacities need to be strengthened and collaboration enhanced among the wide variety of bodies and organizations whose mandates and activities are relevant to addressing the problem of internal displacement; and,

▶ considering the intensity and scope of the crisis of internal displacement, improvements are needed to provide a more predictable and coherent response; the current system of ad hoc collaborative relationships is too often constrained by problems of coordination, neglect of protection and human rights, and insufficient support for the processes of reintegration and development.

The report emphasizes that insufficient attention to protection needs constitutes the greatest gap in existing institutional arrangements. The report furthers notes that the UNHCR and other humanitarian organizations have repeatedly called for the greater involvement of UN human rights bodies in field operations in complex emergencies. Following on this statement, consideration is given to several aspects of the UN's human rights approach in emergencies, including:

▶ deployment of human rights field staff (e.g., in former Yugoslavia and Rwanda) to facilitate information gathering, mediation with local officials, redress of human rights problems, prevention of possible violations, and return of internally displaced persons and refugees by creating conditions of safety in areas of return; and

▶ establishment of a human rights field presence under the programme of advisory services and technical assistance to promote human rights protection through the strengthening of national institutions and enhance efforts to prevent situations which cause or threaten to cause mass exoduses.

The report refers to a number of needs to which field missions and the programmes of advisory services and technical assistance could give greater attention, including:

▶ programmes aimed at the training and strengthening of judicial systems;

▶ involvement in problems related to land, housing, official papers, employment and protection from harassment;

▶ programmes to address the problem of impunity, lack of physical security for the displaced, and issues related to land and property rights; and

▶ expansion of the role of human rights monitors to cover not only the return process but also camp situations.

On the question of return and reintegration, the Representative stated that the inclusion of human rights concerns into projects of return and reintegration is a prerequisite for the development of durable solutions to problems of internal displacement. He urged that such projects include measures specifically addressing the human rights of the internally displaced.

Referring to the situation of women, the Representative stated that, in the course of country visits, he found that the special assistance, protection and development needs experienced by women and children, who constitute the vast majority of the internally displaced, are far from being adequately addressed, both during displacement and during the process of reintegration. The report recalls recommendations previously made to improve the situation of women, including the need to develop measures to ensure that women: are involved in the planning and distribution of relief; are protected against gender-specific violence; and, for women heads of household, that the women receive special training and assistance in becoming economically self-supporting and able to provide for their families. The Representative pointed out that, in many countries, the risk as well as the consequences of losing employment are especially serious for women, who may suffer from double discrimination owing to their ethnicity as well as their gender. They also experience more problems in establishing an alternative source of livelihood since the lack of credit opportunities tends to affect women most severely. These circumstances often compel children in women-headed households to contribute to family income, which, in turn, results in reduced levels of school attendance.

The report concluded by noting that the problem of internal displacement has increased in severity and magnitude in the years since the Representative's mandate was established and stated that this trend is likely to continue.

At its 1997 session, the Commission adopted a resolution by consensus (1997/39) on internally displaced persons. The Commission, *inter alia*: recalled the emphasis in the Vienna Declaration and Programme of Action on the need to develop global strategies to address the problem of internal displacement; reaffirmed that a central coordination mechanism to assign responsibilities in emergency situations is essential; expressed appreciation to relevant entities for provision of assistance and protection to internally displaced persons; recalled that there remain several significant areas in which present international law fails to provide sufficient protection to the internally displaced; encouraged the Representative to continue to develop a comprehensive framework for protection of internally displaced persons; emphasized the need for better implementation of existing international law applicable to the internally displaced; welcomed the attention given by the Representative to the needs of internally displaced women and children and urged him to continue to address these needs; called on governments of countries facing situations of internal displacement that have not yet done so to invite the Representative to conduct a field mission; urged relevant organizations working cooperatively to set up a more comprehensive and coherent system of data collection related to internally displaced persons; welcomed initiatives of regional organizations such as the OSCE and OAU to address the needs of the internally displaced; and, called on the High Commissioner for Human Rights to develop projects to promote the human rights of internally displaced persons and include in a report to the Commission information on their implementation.

The mandate of the Representative on internally displaced persons will be reviewed at the 1998 session of the Commission.

\* \* \* \* \* \* \* \*

# INTERNATIONAL COVENANT ON CIVIL AND POLITICAL RIGHTS

**General Comment by the Human Rights Committee on issues relating to the continuity of obligations to the International Covenant on Civil and Political Rights: Comment 26 (1), adopted at 61st session of the HRC, 29 October 1997 (CCPR/C/21/Rev.1/Add.8/Rev.1)**

The Human Rights Committee, noting that the International Covenant on Civil and Political Rights (ICCPR) contains no provision regarding its termination, or for denunciation or withdrawal from the covenant, concludes that the possibility of termination, denunciation or withdrawal must be considered in light of applicable rules of customary international law which are reflected in the Vienna Convention on the Law of Treaties. On this basis, it concludes that the Covenant is not subject to denunciation or withdrawal unless it is established that the parties intended to admit the possibility of denunciation or withdrawal or that a right to do so is implied from the nature of the treaty. The Committee argues that the

omissions were deliberate and not the result of oversight; and that this is not the type of treaty which, by its nature, implies a right of denunciation. The Committee notes that it has consistently taken the view that the rights enshrined in the Covenant belong to the people living in the territory of the State party. Once the people are accorded the protection of the rights under the Covenant, such protection devolves with territory and continues to belong to them, notwithstanding changes in government of the State party, including dismemberment in more than one state or state succession or any subsequent action of the State party. Therefore, the Committee is firmly of the view that international law does not permit a state which has ratified or acceded or succeeded to the Covenant to denounce it or withdraw from it.

\* \* \* \* \* \* \* \*

# MASS EXODUSES

**Report of the High Commissioner for human rights and mass exoduses (E/CN.4/1997/42)**

The Commission on Human Rights has been considering the question of mass exoduses since 1980 and, up until the 1996 session, had received a report on mass exoduses from the Secretary-General. The 1997 session considered a report prepared by the High Commissioner for Human Rights.

In terms of the main causes of mass exoduses, the report specifically cites international and internal conflicts (at times arising from inter-ethnic violence) and systematic violations of human rights and humanitarian law. The summary of points raised in communications from governments, agencies, NGOs and others on human rights situations affecting refugees and displaced persons highlights a number of areas, including: asylum-related to indifference in some cases and hostility in others to refugees and efforts to convince potential asylum seekers to remain at home; inadequate respect for international human rights standards and norms of refugee law related to voluntary repatriation and the principle of *non-refoulement*; use by immigration officials of deprivation of liberty of children for security or related purposes; and threats and violations of the right to life against refugees and internally displaced persons.

The problems impeding voluntary return are noted as including: an environment of political instability; unsustainable economic conditions; landmines; land and property disputes; violence against those seeking to return or who have returned, including extrajudicial executions, disappearances and torture or ill-treatment; poor health and living conditions in refugee camps; and destruction, looting and occupation of property by others, lack of seeds for planting, collapse of the health care system.

In the section of the report dealing with conclusions and recommendations, the report states that despite the fact that current collaborative arrangements can considerably enhance assistance to and protection of displaced populations, the need for international efforts to go beyond the present system of ad hoc response remains, particularly as regards internally displaced persons. Moreover, a further strengthening of the cooperation between international agencies and the integration of human rights standards in their respective areas of work must be pursued because the emphasis of current inter-agency collaborative efforts often lies in relief assistance rather than protection and, for instance, needs assessment missions only rarely include human rights professionals. The report also observes that the best solution lies in prevention and that, to this end, the inter-agency early-warning efforts should be intensified or resumed, activities in which the High Commissioner should be intimately involved. In addition, the report calls for increased attention to be focussed on the mobilization of a response to early warning signals.

The report concludes with observations on the need to establish the means and will to prevent ethnic conflicts from occurring, strengthen efforts to ensure compliance with international standards related to the protection of civilians in times of armed conflict, address areas related to justice, peace and institution-building in post-conflict reconstruction programmes and adopt a more balanced approach to take advantage of all possibilities for prevention and resolution of crises related to displacement.

At the 1997 session, the Commission adopted a resolution by consensus (1997/75) on the question of human rights and mass exoduses. The Commission, *inter alia*: acknowledged that mass exoduses are caused by multiple factors that may include human rights violations, political, ethnic and economic conflicts, famine, insecurity, violence, poverty and environmental degradation; acknowledged that early warning requires an intersectoral and multidisciplinary approach; recognized the complementarity between protection of human rights and humanitarian action; welcomed existing cooperative initiatives and arrangements; recognized that the UN human rights machinery has important capabilities to address human rights violations causing movements of refugees and displaced persons; recognized that women and children represent the majority of most refugee populations and that women and girls are vulnerable to gender-based discrimination, violence and exploitation; recalled the principles of international protection for refugees; deplored ethnic and other forms of intolerance as one of the major causes of forced migratory movements; urged states to take all necessary steps to ensure respect for the rights of persons belonging to minorities; urged all bodies involved in inter-agency consultations on early warning to cooperate fully and increase the commitment and resources necessary for successful operation of the consultations; invited thematic and country mechanisms and treaty bodies to incorporate into their work information and recommendations on problems resulting in mass exoduses and/or impeding voluntary return; requested the High Commissioner for Human Rights to pay particular attention to situations which cause or threaten to cause mass exoduses and address such situations through protection measures as well as emergency preparedness and response mechanisms; welcomed the establishment by the Department of Humanitarian Affairs of the Humanitarian Early Warning System; urged the Secretary-General to give high priority and the necessary resources to action to identify all human rights abuses that contribute to mass outflows of people and invite comments on the issue; encouraged states that have not done so to ratify or accede to the 1951 Convention relating to the Status of Stateless Persons, the 1961 Convention on the Reduction of Statelessness and other relevant regional refugee instruments and international human rights instruments; called on states to

ensure effective protection for refugees through, *inter alia*, respect for the principle of non-refoulement; and, requested the High Commissioner for Human Rights to submit a report to the 1998 session of the Commission with particular attention paid to defining appropriate early-warning capacities, implementation procedures and activities necessary to respond promptly and effectively.

* * * * * * * *

# MERCENARIES

**Special Rapporteur on the use of mercenaries as a means of impeding the exercise of the right of peoples to self-determination** (E/CN.4/1997/24)

The mandate of the Special Rapporteur (SR) on the use of mercenaries was established in 1987 and was up for renewal at the 1998 session of the Commission. The SR in 1997 was Mr. E. Bernales-Ballesteros (Peru). One of the basic aims of the Commission in establishing the mandate was to encourage states to ratify the International Convention Against the Recruitment, Use, Financing and Training of Mercenaries. However, as of 20 February 1997 only 11 states had become parties to the Convention and only 11 states had signed. Twenty-two ratifications are required for the Convention to enter into force.

The report to the 1997 Commission highlights concerns related to the emergence of private security companies that have been implicated in mercenary activities and the fact that they represent a relatively new operational model. The SR stated that the formal lawfulness of these companies, in the light of the relevant national and international legislation, is not open to question, as they are covered by the gaps and loopholes that would prevent their activities from being classified as mercenary *stricto sensu*. Nonetheless, international allegations about their operations, the concern and alarm of some governments, and the expansion of these firms as a kind of alternative security model for countries with internal conflicts that are practically unmanageable for the governments concerned, make it essential to give some thought to the problem.

Following on this statement, the SR posed a number of questions:

▸ Do mercenaries now constitute the rank and file of personnel recruited by private companies to contract with governments to provide internal security services, safeguard public order, and even put an end to internal armed conflicts?

▸ Is not responsibility for a country's internal order and security an inalienable obligation that a state fulfils through its police and armed forces?

▸ Is it not a serious infringement of a state's sovereignty to hand over such responsibilities to companies registered in third countries?

▸ Who will be responsible for any repressive excesses that may be committed by these companies against the civilian population, particularly with regard to political opposition?

▸ Who will take responsibility for any violations of international humanitarian law or human rights?

▸ Does the international community consider as lawful the existence of a free market for selling security operations if that means that paramilitary forces that incorporate mercenaries can be expected to intervene in a country's internal affairs?

▸ What are the human rights consequences of entrusting internal order and control over civil rights to an international private security firm?

▸ Is the international community willing to accept and concur with the idea that the illegality of recruitment of mercenaries is applied only in very few limited cases?

▸ When and under what circumstances can the recruitment, financing and/or use of mercenaries be considered legal and legitimate?

Arising from these questions, the report states that the ambiguity of existing provisions, the gaps in national legislation, and the insecurity which prevails in many countries, as well as the end-of-century tendency to privatize everything in sight, have created the conditions for the establishment of this new type of company. Such companies are organized to sell security in the international market to client countries from which they obtains contracts worth millions, protection, and links to powerful companies dealing in oil, minerals and precious stones. The results are the growth and expansion of these companies and their presence in the countries with which the contractual relationship has been established. The SR did not claim that all military and police advisory assistance provided by foreigners or private foreign companies is illegal and contrary to the sovereignty of a state. He acknowledged that such advisory services do exist and, when clearly demarcated, are not contrary to international law or national constitutional provisions. The intent of the report was to draw attention to the dangerous grey areas and the limits which need legal safeguards in order to prohibit such advisory services from becoming active armed participation in internal conflicts or in matters of the internal security of citizens that are connected with the exercise of the rights and political freedoms provided for in international human rights instruments.

The report concludes with a number of recommendations, including that:

▸ the Commission on Human Rights reaffirm its condemnation of mercenary activities;

▸ the international community take adequate account of the link between terrorism and mercenary activities and the participation of mercenaries in criminal acts of a terrorist nature;

▸ commissions and working groups considering the question of terrorism include mercenary activities in analysis and conclusions;

▸ the Commission urge states to adopt legislation prohibiting mercenary activity;

▸ the Commission appeal to states to ratify or accede to the Convention so that it may come into force; and

▸ the Commission closely monitor the evolution of private legally registered companies as well as developments in national legislation and terms under which some states conclude contracts with such companies.

As happened in 1996, the 1997 session of the Commission did not adopt a resolution on the question of the use of mercenaries.

*  *  *  *  *  *  *  *

# RACIAL DISCRIMINATION

**Special Rapporteur on contemporary forms of racism, racial discrimination, xenophobia and related intolerance** (E/CN.4/1997/71; A/52/471)

The mandate of the Special Rapporteur (SR) was created in 1993 and renewed for a further three years by the Commission at its 1996 session. In 1997, the SR was Mr. Glele-Ahanhanzo (Benin). The main focus of the Special Rapporteur's work has been and continues to be contemporary forms of racism, racial discrimination, any form of discrimination against Blacks, Arabs and Muslims, xenophobia, negrophobia, anti-Semitism, and related intolerance. To date, the main reports of the SR have emphasized education programs to promote tolerance.

The 1997 report includes summary sections on various "target groups" which are victims of racism and racist attitudes. On the subject of negrophobia and discrimination against Blacks, the report notes the use of the Internet to spread racist messages. There are two recommendations in the report. The first is that the United Nations convene a world conference on racism, racial discrimination and xenophobia, with the question of immigration and xenophobia included on the agenda. The second is that there be action at the international level, in the form of studies, research and immediate joint action to respond to the use of the Internet as a vehicle for racist propaganda.

The section of the report addressing anti-Semitism reproduced portions of a study on anti-Semitism throughout the world in 1995 (1997/71, para. 27, section 3). The study, which included commentary on the decline in violent acts, the Jewish stereotype, Islamist and Arab anti-Semitism, and anti-Semitism on the Internet, was prepared by the University of Tel Aviv and forwarded to the SR by the Israeli government. In the report there was a paragraph which read:

One might say that while part of anti-Semitism in Christian countries in recent decades has become anti-Zionism, in the Muslim world anti-Zionism appears to be turning into anti-Jewish manifestations, thus broadening a political and territorial conflict into a clash between ideological and religious world views. The use of Christian and secular European anti-Semitism motifs in Muslim publications is on the rise, yet at the same time Muslim extremists are turning increasingly to their own religious sources, first and foremost the Qur'an, as a primary anti-Jewish source.

The inclusion of this statement was protested by a number of governments on the basis that it is an insult to Islam; the assertion is tantamount to blasphemy; the statement refers to religion and therefore should not and cannot be properly included in a report by a mechanism for which the mandate relates to racism; the statement incites hostility towards Arabs and Islam; and the statement ignores the fact that Arabs are Semites. The protesting states called for the deletion of the offending reference from the report and a statement of censure by the Commission. Extended negotiations resulted in the Commission deciding to: express its indignation and protest at the content of such an offensive reference to Islam and the Qur'an; affirm that the offensive reference should have been excluded from the report; and request the Chairman of the Commission to ask the SR to take corrective action in response to the Commission's decision.

Renewal of the mandate on racism and racial discrimination will be considered by the Commission at its 1999 session.

At its 1997 session the Commission adopted two resolutions, both by consensus, on the subject of racism and racial discrimination. The texts are virtually identical in a number of respects. The fact that two resolutions were adopted reflected the inability of the Commission to negotiate a comprehensive text incorporating all elements, including the decision to request that the United Nations hold a world conference on racism by the year 2001.

In the first resolution (1997/73) the Commission, *inter alia*: expressed concern that acts against Blacks, Arabs and Muslims, xenophobia, negrophobia, anti-Semitism persist and take new forms and include tendencies to establish policies based racial, religious, ethnic, cultural and national superiority or exclusivity; recognized the distinction between racism as an institutionalized governmental policy, or arising from official doctrines of racial superiority, and manifestations of racism and acts perpetrated by individuals or groups; noted general recommendation XV (42) of 17 March 1993 by the Committee on the Elimination of Racial Discrimination, holding that the prohibition of dissemination of all ideas based on racial superiority or racial hatred is compatible with the right to freedom of opinion and expression as set out in article 19 of the Universal Declaration and article 5 of the Convention on the Elimination of All Forms of Racial Discrimination; noted that manifestations of racism and xenophobia are taking increasingly violent forms; reaffirmed that impunity for crimes motivated by racist or xenophobic attitudes contributes to a weakening of rule of law and tends to encourage the recurrence of such crimes; expressed support and appreciation for the work of the SR and its continuation; unequivocally condemned all forms of racism, racial discrimination and all racist acts and, in particular, racist violence and related acts of random and indiscriminate violence; condemned manifestations of racism and intolerance against migrant workers and members of their families and other vulnerable groups in societies; categorically condemned any role played by some print, audiovisual or electronic media in inciting acts of violence motivated by racial hatred; welcomed the designation by the European Union of 1997 as the European Year against Racism; called on states to enact and enforce legislation to prevent and sanction acts of racism and racial discrimination; recommended that states give priority to education as a means of preventing and eradicating racism; welcomed the active role of NGOs in combatting racism and assisting victims of racist acts; and, urged all governments to cooperate fully with the SR; and invited all governments to provide assistance and rehabilitation to victims of racist acts and related intolerances.

The second resolution adopted by the Commission (1997/74) was divided into six sections.

In Section I (General), the CHR: unequivocally condemned all forms of racism and racial discrimination, including racist and related acts of random and indiscriminate violence; declared racism and racial discrimination to be among the most serious violations of human rights; underlined the importance of effective action to foster harmony and tolerance within societies; condemned manifestations of racism and intolerance against migrant workers; condemned the role played by print, audio-visual or electronic media in inciting acts of violence motivated by racial hatred; noted with interest general recommendation XV (42) of the Committee on the Elimination of Racial Discrimination regarding the compatibility of the prohibition on dissemination of all ideas based on racial superiority or racial hatred and the rights set out in article 19 of the Universal Declaration of Human Rights and article 5 of the Convention on the Elimination of All Forms of Racial Discrimination;

In Section II (The Third Decade to Combat Racism), the CHR: regretted the lack of interest, support and financial resources for the Programme of Action for the Third Decade to Combat Racism and Racial Discrimination; expressed the view that donations to the Trust Fund have proved inadequate and that the General Assembly should consider ways and means of financing the Programme, including through the UN regular budget; invited the General Assembly to consider the possibility of providing the resources required for implementation; called on governments, UN bodies, agencies, intergovernmental organizations and NGOs to participate in the Third Decade; requested the High Commissioner for Human Rights to give due attention to appeals by the General Assembly and ECOSOC to establish a mechanism within Office of the High Commissioner for Human Rights (OHCHR) as a focal point for coordinating activities related to the Third Decade; reaffirmed the General Assembly recommendation that a seminar be organized by the OHCHR and other appropriate entities to assess the role of the Internet; recommended that states give priority to education as a means to prevent and eradicate racism and related intolerance; encouraged mass media to promote ideas of tolerance and understanding among peoples and between cultures;

In Section III (Follow-up Activities), the CHR: welcomed publication by the Centre for Human Rights of "Model Legislation for the Guidance of Governments in the Enactment of Further Legislation against Racial Discrimination"; invited states to ensure that the competence of institutions related to the protection and promotion of human rights encompasses issues linked to the fight against racism and racial discrimination; recommended that celebrations of the 50th anniversary of the Universal Declaration include programs targeted at combatting racism and racial discrimination;

In Section IV (Special Rapporteur), the CHR: took note of the reports of the Special Rapporteur (SR) and expressed full support and appreciation for the work undertaken and for its continuation; urged all governments to cooperate fully with the SR; invited governments of countries visited by the SR to consider ways to implement the recommendations arising from those visits and to permit follow-up visits if necessary; urged the High Commissioner for Human Rights to provide, at their request, technical services to governments seeking to implement the recommendations of the SR;

In Section V (on the Convention on racial discrimination), the CHR: appealed to states that have not done so to consider ratifying and acceding to the Convention; encouraged states to limit the extent of any reservations entered and to formulate reservations as narrowly as possible; called on states parties to adopt measures immediately aimed at elimination of all forms of racial discrimination; requested states parties that have not done so to consider making a declaration under article 14 (individual complaints procedure); and;

In Section VI (World Conference on Racism), the CHR: recommended to the General Assembly the convening of a world conference on racism and racial discrimination, xenophobia and related intolerance, with the following main objectives: (a) to review progress made in the fight against racism and reappraise obstacles to further progress and ways to overcome them; (b) to consider ways and means better to ensure application of existing standards and implementation of existing relevant instruments; (c) to increase the level of awareness about the prevalence of racism and racial discrimination, xenophobia and related intolerance; (d) to formulate concrete recommendations on ways to increase the effectiveness of activities and mechanisms of the UN to combat racism, racial discrimination, xenophobia and related intolerance; (e) to review the political, historic, economic, social, cultural and any other factors leading to racism and related intolerance; (f) to formulate concrete recommendations to further action-oriented national, regional and international measures to combat all forms of racism and related intolerance; (g) draw up concrete recommendations to ensure that the UN has the financial and other necessary resources for its action to combat racism and related intolerance; recommended that the world conference be convened not later than the year 2001; recommended that the General Assembly, in considering a draft agenda for the world conference, take into account the need to address in a comprehensive manner all forms of racism, racial discrimination, xenophobia and related contemporary forms of intolerance; stressed the importance of taking into account a gender perspective systematically throughout preparation of the conference; recommended that the world conference be action-oriented and focus on practical measures to eradicate racism, including through measures of prevention, education and protection and provision of effective remedies; recommended that the Commission on Human Rights act as the preparatory committee for the world conference and that its deliberations be open-ended; requested governments, agencies, bodies and organizations, including NGOs, to submit recommendations concerning the conference and preparations for it and to participate actively in the conference; recommended that the General Assembly: (a) call on states and regional organizations to hold national or regional meetings or take other measures to prepare for the conference; and, (b) request regional meetings to submit reports to the preparatory committee on the outcome of their deliberations.

* * * * * * * *

# RELIGIOUS INTOLERANCE

### Special Rapporteur on religious intolerance
(E/CN.4/1997/91; A/52/477)

The mandate of the Special Rapporteur (SR) on religious intolerance was created by the Commission in 1986 and given the specific task of identifying incidents and government actions that are inconsistent with provisions in the Declaration on the Elimination of all Forms of Intolerance and of Discrimination Based on Religion or Belief. The SR was also requested to make recommendations on remedial measures that should be taken to ensure compliance by states with the provisions of the Declaration. In 1997, the SR was Mr. Abdelfattah Amor (Tunisia).

The report to the 1997 Commission notes that the Special Rapporteur had addressed communications to governments alleging problems or violations related to religious intolerance affecting a number of religions, religious groups and religious communities, including: Christianity, Islam, Buddhism, Hinduism, Judaism, Baha'is, Jehovah's Witnesses, Hare Krishna, Al Arqam, Darul Arqam, Mormons, Navajos (Dine) and Apaches. The allegations arose from various concerns, including discriminatory policies, laws and/or regulations related to religion or belief, religious extremism, violations of freedom of thought, conscience and religion or belief, violations of the freedom to manifest one's religion or belief, freedom to dispose of religious property and violations of the right to life, physical integrity and health.

The section of the report dealing with conclusions and recommendations considers aspects of religious freedom arising from the rights to change religion and conscientious objection. Commentary is also provided on religious freedom and human rights, religion and politics, religious freedom and religious extremism and religious freedom and sects. The recommendations drawn from these considerations include that:

▸ a high-level governmental meeting agree upon a collective approach to sects and religions that respects human rights;

▸ the Commission mandate a study on the phenomena of sects and religious freedom; and

▸ a department on religious freedom and human rights be established within the Office of the High Commissioner for Human Rights to increase, channel and target information on the religious situation around the world, leading to the creation of a database to enable more thorough analysis and investigation in the area of religious freedom.

The Commission will consider renewal of the mandate on religious intolerance in 1998.

At its 1997 session, the Commission adopted a resolution on religious intolerance (1997/18) by consensus. The Commission, *inter alia*: emphasized that the right to freedom of thought, conscience, religion and belief is far-reaching and encompasses freedom of thought on all matters, personal conviction and commitment to religion or belief manifested either individually or in community with others; condemned all forms of intolerance and discrimination based on religion or belief; urged states to ensure that constitutional and legal frameworks provide adequate protections for rights related to thought, conscience, religion and belief; urged states to ensure that no one within their jurisdiction is deprived of the rights to life, liberty and security of person because of religion or belief or is subjected to torture or arbitrary arrest or detention on that account; urged states to take all necessary steps to combat hatred, intolerance and violence, intimidation and coercion arising from religion intolerance, including practices which violate women's human rights and discriminate against women; urged states to ensure that members of law enforcement bodies and civil servants, educators and other public officials respect different religions and beliefs and do not discriminate on religious grounds; urged states to ensure that religious places, sites and shrines are fully respected and protected; emphasized the view of the Human Rights Committee that restrictions on freedom to manifest religion or belief are permitted only if limitations are prescribed by law, necessary to public safety, order, health or morals and are applied in a manner that does not vitiate the right to freedom of thought, conscience or belief; encouraged the SR to continue efforts to examine incidents and governmental actions that are incompatible with provisions of the Declaration and recommend remedial measures as appropriate; stressed the need for the SR to apply a gender perspective in the reporting process through identification of gender-specific abuses; called on governments to cooperate with the SR and consider extending invitations to him to conduct visits; and, considered it desirable to increase UN promotional and public information activities in areas related to freedom of religion or belief, including the widest dissemination possible of the text of the Declaration by UN information centres.

\* \* \* \* \* \* \* \*

# TORTURE

### Special Rapporteur on Torture (E/CN.4/1997/7; E/CN.4/1997/7/Add.1)

The Commission established the mandate of the Special Rapporteur (SR) on the question of torture at its 1985 session and has renewed it as required since then. In 1997, the SR was Mr. Nigel Rodley (UK). At the 1998 session, the Commission will consider renewal of the mandate for a further three years.

The focus of the work of the SR is primarily torture, but there is scope within the mandate to consider cases within a "grey zone" related to other forms of cruel, inhuman and degrading treatment or punishment. In recent years, the use of corporal punishment has been considered to fall within this "grey zone" and the SR has taken up the issue of, and cases related to, such practices as: flagellation; stoning; amputation of ears, fingers, toes or limbs; and branding or tattooing. The report notes that, with respect to the practice in some countries, the authority for the imposition and execution of the punishment derives from legislation or executive decree having the force of legislation. The legal provisions in question envisage the infliction of corporal punishment as an ordinary criminal sanction, either as an alternative to or in combination with other sanctions such as a fine or imprisonment. In some countries the provisions are to be found in administrative regulations, such as that contained in prison manuals in respect of disciplinary offences. In other instances, informal

or quasi-official agencies, such as ad hoc village tribunals or religious courts, have pronounced sentences of corporal punishment which appear to be extrinsic to the state's constitutional criminal justice system. In respect of these latter cases, the state must be considered responsible for the consequences of these sentences if they are carried out with its authorization, consent or acquiescence.

The report notes that a small number of governments and some legal experts base their opinion that corporal punishment should not be considered to be torture or cruel, inhuman or degrading treatment or punishment on the provision in article 1 of the Convention against Torture. This article defines torture for the purposes of the Convention and excludes from the ambit of proscribed acts those resulting in "pain or suffering arising only from, inherent in or incidental to lawful sanctions." The report goes on to note the SR's disagreement with this interpretation of article 1, and states that lawful sanctions must necessarily refer to those sanctions that constitute practices widely accepted as legitimate by the international community.

The two reports provided to the Commission in 1997 do not include any additional recommendations to those made in previous years. Among other things, those recommendations called for:

▸ the definition and designation of torture as a specific crime in national legislation;

▸ inadmissibility to judicial proceedings of any evidence obtained through torture;

▸ abolition of secret places of detention;

▸ inadmissibility to judicial proceedings of any evidence obtained from a detainee in such a place;

▸ regular inspection by independent experts of places of detention, including police lock-ups, pre-trial detention centres, security services premises and administrative detention areas and prisons, and a public report of the findings of the experts;

▸ prohibition of incommunicado detention;

▸ access for detainees to legal counsel within 24 hours of detention;

▸ the same degree of protection for persons under administrative detention as that accorded to those under criminal detention;

▸ guarantee of habeas corpus and *amparo* to ensure the right of all persons to challenge the lawfulness of detention;

▸ investigation of all complaints of torture and, if considered valid, compensation for the victims or their relatives;

▸ abrogation of amnesties, indemnity laws and other means of exemption from criminal responsibility for torturers;

▸ implementation of strict measures against medical personnel who play a role in torture, be that role direct or indirect; and

▸ inclusion in national legislation of the principle of article 3 of the Convention against Torture, related to prohibition on expulsion, return or extradition of a person to another state where there exists substantial grounds to believe that torture will occur.

In addition to a resolution adopted on the question of the draft optional protocol to the Convention against Torture (1997/24) the Commission adopted a resolution by consensus on the question of torture and the mandate of the Special Rapporteur (1997/38). The Commission, *inter alia*: urged all states to become parties to Convention against Torture; invited all states parties to make declarations under articles 21 and 22 (inter-state and individual complaints procedures); called on all governments to implement fully the prohibition on torture and other cruel treatment or punishment; urged all governments to promote the implementation of the Vienna Declaration and Programme of Action, in particular Part II, section B.5, related to freedom from torture; stressed that under international law acts of torture must be made offences under domestic criminal law; reminded governments that corporal punishment can amount to cruel, inhuman or degrading treatment or punishment; stressed that all allegations of torture should be promptly examined by an impartial and competent national authority; stressed that those who encourage, order, tolerate or perpetrate torture and related acts must be held responsible and punished; emphasized the obligation of states parties to the Convention to provide training for personnel who may be involved in custody, interrogation or treatment of persons under any form of arrest, detention or imprisonment; stressed that states must not punish individuals for refusing orders to commit acts amounting to torture or related acts; welcomed the work of Committee against Torture and its practice of formulating concluding observations after consideration of reports as well as the practice of carrying out inquiries into cases indicating a systematic practice of torture in states parties to the Convention; requested the General Assembly to proclaim 26 June as the UN international day in support of victims of torture and the total eradication of torture; commended the SR for his work as reflected in his report; recalled recommendations made in previous reports; reminded states that prolonged incommunicado detention may perpetuate torture and can itself be a form of cruel; inhuman or degrading treatment; invited the SR to continue examining questions related to torture directed against women and conditions conducive to such torture, to make recommendations concerning the prevention and redress of gender-specific forms of torture, and to exchange views with the SR on violence against women with a view to greater mutual effectiveness and cooperation; invited the SR to continue consideration of questions related to the torture of children and to make appropriate recommendations; approved the methods of work employed by the SR, in particular urgent appeals; called on all governments to cooperate with and assist the SR; encouraged all governments to consider inviting the SR to visit their countries; noted the report on the Voluntary Fund for Victims of Torture; appealed to all governments, organizations and individuals to contribute annually to the Fund; stressed the need for contributions to the Fund on a regular basis; stressed the increasing demand for assistance to rehabilitation services for victims of torture; and, urged states in arrears on funding the Committee against Torture (pre-dating the decision to fund from the UN regular budget) to fulfil their financial obligations immediately.

**General Comment by the Committee against Torture (CAT) on the Implementation of Article 3 in the context of Article 22 of the Convention**

The CAT, at its 19th session (on 21 November 1997), adopted a General Comment for the guidance of States parties to the Convention and authors of communications in the context of Article 22 (on the admissibility of communications).

The CAT noted that Article 3 — "No state Party shall expel, return *("refouler")* or extradite a person to another State where there are substantial grounds for believing that he would be in danger of being subjected to torture" — is confined in its application to cases where there are substantial grounds for believing that the author would be in danger of being subjected to torture as defined in Article 1 of the Convention. Further, that in paragraph 2 of article 3 — which states that "For the purpose of determining whether there are such grounds, the competent authorities shall take into account all relevant considerations including, where applicable, the existence in the State concerned of a consistent pattern of gross, flagrant or mass violations of human rights" — the phrase "the State concerned" refers to the state to which the individual concerned is being expelled, returned or extradited, as well as to any state to which the author may subsequently be expelled, returned or extradited; and that "a consistent pattern of gross, flagrant or mass violations of human rights" refers only to violations by or at the instigation of or with the consent or acquiescence of a public official or other person acting in an official capacity.

The Committee is of the opinion that it is the responsibility of the author to establish a *prima facie* case for the purpose of admissibility of his or her communication; and that, with respect to the merits of a case, the burden is upon the author to present an arguable case, i.e., there must be a factual basis for the author's position sufficient to require a response from the State party. When the CAT assesses the risk of torture, it must go beyond mere theory or suspicion, although the risk does not have to meet the test of high probability. "The author must establish that he/she would be in danger of being tortured and that the grounds for so believing are substantial in the way described, and that such danger is personal and present." The CAT then provides a list of what information would be pertinent to establishing such a danger.

* * * * * * * *

# TOXIC AND DANGEROUS PRODUCTS AND WASTES

**Special Rapporteur on the illicit movement and dumping of toxic and dangerous products and wastes (E/CN.4/1997/19)**

The 1995 decision of the Commission to establish this mandate (Resolution 1995/81) was not made by consensus and the resolutions adopted in subsequent years have not enjoyed the support of the full Commission. Opposition has largely been based on the argument that the subject is not one the Commission can handle effectively and that the issue is better addressed through the mechanisms associated with the 1989 Basel Convention on the Control of Transboundary Movements of Hazardous Wastes and their Disposal. In 1997, the Special Rapporteur (SR) was Ms. F.Z. Ksentini (Algeria). The mandate of the SR has four components:

▸ investigation and examination of the effects of illicit dumping of toxic wastes and products in African and other developing countries, with particular attention paid to effects on the rights to life and health;

▸ receipt of information on the illicit traffic and dumping of such wastes and products in African and other developing countries;

▸ recommendations and/or proposals for measures to control, reduce and eradicate this illicit traffic in, transfer to and dumping of such products in African and other developing countries; and

▸ production annually of a list of countries and transnational corporations engaged in the illicit dumping of toxic wastes and products in African and other developing countries as well as production of a census of persons killed, maimed or otherwise injured in developing countries through this practice.

The 1997 report includes a summary of the general views of some governments on both the mandate and the issue, while a significant number of the commentaries in other parts of the report relate to issues and practices of a bilateral nature. The incidents and situations summarized in the report include: a case of the leakage of toxic gas; the export of battery scrap from developed to developing countries; mining waste spills and environmental degradation (including the destruction of rain forests) related to mining, oil drilling and the building of gas pipelines; military operations and forced labour related to oil and gas exploitation; a fire and explosion related to the importation and abandonment of hazardous chemicals and wastes; environmental pollution from power plants; pollution from the manufacture of herbicides in developing countries; and nuclear contamination of the environment.

The report prompted many objections from governments of both developed and developing countries on a number of grounds, including that: the information did not relate to illegal activities; the information related to situations and incidents that were common or had occurred prior to 1995 when the mandate was established; and that it referred to situations for which remedial measures had already been taken and/or was out-of-date and/or incomplete. In response to the objections to her methods of work, the SR defended her decision to include this information on the grounds that, while not strictly illegal, these practices are "illicit" in the sense that they are or should be the subject of disapproval or prohibition for moral or ethical reasons.

Renewal of the mandate for a further three years will be discussed at the 1998 session of the Commission.

At its 1997session, the Commission adopted a resolution on this subject (1997/9) by roll call vote. The Commission, *inter alia*: expressed awareness of the increasing rate of dumping in African and other developing countries by transnational corporations and other enterprises from industrialized countries; acknowledged that many developing countries do not have national capacities and technologies to process toxic wastes and products without an adverse effect on life and health; noted the report of the Special Rapporteur; condemned the increasing rate of dumping; reaffirmed that the practice constitutes a serious threat to the rights to life and health; urged all governments to take legislative and other measures to prevent illegal international trafficking in such products and wastes; invited the United Nations Environmental Programme (UNEP), the Secretariat of the Basel

Convention, the International Labour Office (ILO), the World Health Organization (WHO), the International Atomic Energy Agency (IAEA), the Organization of African Unity (OAU) and other regional organizations to intensify cooperation on environmentally sound management of toxic chemicals and hazardous wastes, including their transboundary movement; requested the SR to undertake within her mandate a global, multi-disciplinary and comprehensive study of existing problems of and solutions to illicit traffic, transfer and dumping of such products and wastes in Africa and other developing countries; requested the SR to include in her 1998 report recommendations and proposals on adequate measures to control, reduce and eradicate the practices; repeated its request to the SR to include in the 1998 report, in a manner consistent with her mandate, information on countries and enterprises engaged in illicit movement of such products; requested the SR in accordance with her mandate to include in the report comprehensive information on persons killed, maimed or otherwise injured in developing countries as a result of these practices; and, encouraged the SR to provide governments with an appropriate opportunity to respond to allegations received by her and reflected in her report.

* * * * * * * *

# WOMEN

**Special Rapporteur on violence against women, its causes and consequences** (E/CN.4/1997/47; E/CN.4/1997/47/Add.4)

The mandate of the Special Rapporteur (SR) on violence against women, its causes and consequences, was established by the Commission at its 1994 session and renewed at the 1997 session. Renewal of the mandate will be considered again at the Commission's session in the year 2000. In 1997, the SR was Ms. Radhika Coomaraswamy.

The mandate is defined by three broad categories: violence in the family (domestic violence), violence in the community and violence in the context of armed conflict. The normative framework through which the mandate is approached is established by the International Covenants on Human Rights, the Convention on the Elimination of All Forms of Discrimination against Women and the Declaration on the Elimination of Violence against Women.

The 1997 main report focusses on violence against women in the community. "Community" is understood to be a social space outside the family but not fully under the control of the state. It is the site for flourishing private organizations and intermediary associations which have an impact on the lives of women as part of their daily interactions and may also be the site of restrictions on and regulations of female sexuality. The SR states that a key component of community identity, and therefore the demarcation of community boundaries, is the preservation of communal honour. Such honour is frequently perceived by both community and non-community members as residing in the sexual behaviour of the women of the community. Communities, therefore, "police" the behaviour of their female members.

The report includes sections on rape and sexual violence, including sexual harassment, trafficking in women and forced prostitution, violence against women migrant workers, and religious extremism. On these points, the recommendations in the report include that:

▸ states amend penal codes so that victim-centred definitions of rape are broad enough to cover the full range of sexual violence and sensitive enough to respond to the possible "consent" of the victim;

▸ sentencing structures be amended to ensure that perpetrators of violence are duly punished and that perpetrators of aggravated crimes receive severe sentences;

▸ states criminalize sexual harassment;

▸ legislation and institutions related to equality in educational institutions and the workplace make provision for combatting sexual harassment;

▸ organizations and institutions providing education and employment ensure that women victims of sexual harassment receive a proper hearing and that there is due process of law;

▸ states assess rules of evidence from a gender perspective and revise evidentiary rules where laws discriminate against women — e.g., laws requiring corroboration because the victim is a woman or those that allow past sexual conduct to be revealed in court even though it has no relevance to the case being heard;

▸ states provide legal mechanisms for protecting a rape victim's identity and privacy during investigations and prosecutions;

▸ judicial constructions such as corroboration and the "honour defence" be reviewed and legislated against if they discriminate against or demean women;

▸ states implement gender-sensitization and awareness-raising programs at all levels of the police and judiciary;

▸ states incorporate changes in school curricula to create attitudes to help combat violence against women;

▸ states incorporate mandatory gender-sensitization training in medical and legal education;

▸ states implement gender-sensitization and awareness training for medical personnel working with victims of rape and other forms of violence against women, with particular attention given to training for state forensic pathologists;

▸ states, in collaboration with non-governmental organizations, allocate funds for victim support services;

▸ restrictions on access to abortion be lifted in cases of rape;

▸ states take steps towards widening women's access to safe and legal abortions;

▸ the international community begin a dialogue aimed at establishing new international standards with regard to trafficking and prostitution;

▸ states initiate special efforts to address international trafficking in women, including through regular exchange of information among police and the judiciary in countries affected by such trafficking;

▸ receiving states revise immigration policies to prevent vulnerable women from being doubly marginalized;

▸ procedures be put in place to ensure that traffickers cannot act with impunity because of the immediate deportation of trafficked women;

▸ social policies be constructed to ensure that marginalized women are given avenues other than prostitution for their vocations and livelihood;

▸ states ensure that police and the judiciary are sensitized to issues and responsive to the magnitude of the social problem, especially as this relates to denigrating attitudes that may hinder criminal prosecution of those who traffic in women;

▸ states, in collaboration with non-governmental organizations, ensure that special services are available to women victims of trafficking and prostitution;

▸ states strengthen programs related to health education, including awareness-raising on HIV/AIDS;

▸ health facilities be responsive to the general needs of women victims with regard to sexually transmitted diseases;

▸ states develop a mechanism to combat complicity by police and immigration officers in the process of trafficking and forced prostitution of women;

▸ all states ratify the Convention on the Protection of the Rights of All Migrant Workers and Members of Their Families;

▸ sending states establish migrant desks at embassies or consulates to assist migrant workers and particularly those who are victims of violence;

▸ sending states implement orientation programs for migrant workers, including basic language skills, an introduction to the culture in which they will be living, and information on what to do in situations of violence;

▸ receiving states prosecute employers who abuse women migrant workers;

▸ receiving states, in collaboration with non-governmental organizations, ensure that shelters and counselling services are available for women migrant workers who are victims of violence;

▸ receiving states combat racist laws and attitudes that dehumanize immigrant populations;

▸ states adhere to commitments in the Declaration on the Elimination of Violence against Women and not invoke custom, religion or tradition to justify violence against women;

▸ laws which prevent effective prosecution of rape and domestic violence sanctioned by religious interpretations be repealed;

▸ states ensure that traditional practices and rituals in the community with violate women's human rights are eliminated;

▸ all violations of women's reproductive health be recognized and eliminated;

▸ states adopt legislation regulating prenatal sex determination to eliminate discriminatory abortions of female foetuses;

► customs and practices promoting son preference and encouraging sex-selective abortions and female infanticide be eliminated;

► studies be commissioned to assess the impact of new technology on violence against women;

► strategies be developed to combat images perpetuating violence against women, without violating freedom of speech and expression;

► the concept of hate speech be developed so that speech and expression which are violent and abusive to women become unacceptable in the community; and

► educational curricula be revised in order to develop sensitive attitudes with regard to violence against women at an early stage of children's development.

On the issue of state responsibility for non-state actors and the basis upon which UN human rights mechanisms may or may not consider abuses by non-state entities and individuals, the SR recalls that, in the past, a strict interpretation of human rights law considered that the state is only responsible for its own actions or that of its agents, and that action by private actors is a matter of criminal justice. In recent times, however, this approach has given way to more realist thinking which holds that states are expected to exercise due diligence in preventing, prosecuting and punishing those who perpetrate violence against women, whether those acts are perpetrated by the state or by private actors. Following on this, the SR reasserted that the emergence of state responsibility for violence in society plays an absolutely crucial role in efforts to eradicate gender-based violence and is perhaps one of the most important contributions of the women's movement to the issue of human rights.

### Resolutions of the Commission on Human Rights

At its 1997 session, the Commission adopted by consensus a number of resolutions on women's human rights generally. Three resolutions addressed the issue of violence against women and one addressed integrating women's human rights throughout the UN system.

### Violence against Women

In the first, on the elimination of violence against women (1997/44), the Commission, *inter alia*: welcomed the adoption, in 1993, of the Declaration on the Elimination of Violence against Women; recalled that the Vienna Declaration and Programme of Action reaffirmed that gender-based violence and all forms of sexual harassment and exploitation must be eradicated; expressed concern that some women are particularly vulnerable to violence, including those belonging to minorities, indigenous women, refugees, migrants, women living in rural or remote communities, women living in destitution, elderly women, women in situations of armed conflict, and girls and women in institutions or detention; expressed alarm at the increase of sexual violence against women and children in situations of armed conflict and reiterated that such acts are grave breaches of international humanitarian law; welcomed progress achieved in the Beijing concluding document in some areas such as violence against women, women and armed conflict and women's human rights; stressed the importance of working towards the elimination of violence against women in public and private life;

commended the SR for her analysis of violence in the family and community; emphasized the duty of governments to refrain from engaging in violence against women and to exercise due diligence to prevent, investigate and punish acts of violence against women, whether perpetrated by the state or by private persons; emphasized the duty of governments to provide access to just and effective remedies and specialized assistance to victims; condemned all violations of women's human rights in situations of armed conflict and recognized them as violations of international human rights and humanitarian law; called for a particularly effective response to violations in situations of armed conflict and particularly murder, systematic rape, sexual slavery and forced pregnancy; encouraged states participating in the drafting of the statute for the International Criminal Court to give full consideration to integrating a gender perspective; requested all governments to cooperate with and assist the SR; requested human rights treaty bodies and other special rapporteurs, UN entities, intergovernmental and non-governmental organizations to cooperate with and assist the SR; stressed the conclusion of the SR that states have a positive duty to promote and protect women's human rights and exercise due diligence; called on states to ratify and/or implement international human rights norms and instruments as they relate to violence against women; called on states to include in their reports to treaty bodies gender-disaggregated information and information on violence against women, and measures to implement the Beijing concluding document; called on states to condemn violence against women and not invoke custom, tradition or practices in the name of religion to avoid obligations to eliminate such violence; called on states to take action to eradicate violence in the family and community; called on states to enact and/or enforce penal, civil, labour and administrative sanctions to punish and redress wrongs done to women and girls subjected to any form of violence; called on states to enact and/or enforce legislation protecting girls from all forms of violence, including female infanticide, prenatal sex selection, genital mutilation, incest, sexual abuse, sexual exploitation, child prostitution and child pornography; called on states to develop age-appropriate safe and confidential programs and medical, social and psychological support services to assist girls subjected to violence; called on states to establish and carry out training programs for judicial, legal, medical, social, education, police and immigration personnel; called on states to enact and/or enforce legislation to ensure effective protection against rape, sexual harassment and all other forms of violence; called on states that are not parties to the Women's Convention (CEDAW) to work actively towards ratification of or accession to it so that universal ratification can be achieved by year 2000; and, continued the mandate of the Special Rapporteur for a further three years.

### Violence against Women Migrant Workers

The second resolution (1997/13) was partially based on the 1996 report of the Secretary-General (A/51/325) on violence against women migrant workers. The Commission, *inter alia*: noted that women migrant workers seek employment abroad because of poverty, unemployment in their home country and other socio-economic conditions; acknowledged the duty of sending states to work for conditions that provide employment and security to their citizens; expressed concern at reports of abuses and violence committed against women migrant workers by some employers in host countries; acknowledged measures adopted by some receiving states to improve the situation of women migrant workers living in their jurisdiction; encouraged states to enact or reinforce penal, civil, labour and administrative sanctions to punish and redress wrongs done to women whether in the home, workplace, community or society; encouraged states to adopt and/or implement and periodically review laws to ensure the effective elimination of violence against women; encouraged states to take measures to ensure protection of women subjected to violence and access to just and effective remedies, including compensation, indemnification and rehabilitation; invited states to consider adopting appropriate legal measures against intermediaries who deliberately encourage clandestine movement of workers and exploit women migrant workers; reiterated the need for states to conduct regular consultations to identify problem areas in the promotion and protection of the rights of women migrant workers and ensuring health, legal and social services for them; and, encouraged states to consider signing and ratifying or acceding to the International Convention on the Protection of the Rights of All Migrant Workers and Members of Their Families as well as the 1926 Slavery Convention.

**Traffic in Women and Girls**

The third resolution (1997/19) addressed the issue of traffic in women and girls. The Commission, *inter alia*: noted with concern the increasing number of women and girls from developing countries and some countries with economies in transition being victimized by traffickers; acknowledged that trafficking also victimizes young boys; acknowledged the need for adoption of effective measures nationally, regionally and internationally to protect women and girls from trafficking; called on states of origin, transit and destination to consider ratification and enforcement of international conventions on trafficking in persons and on slavery; called on those states to take measures to address root factors, including external ones, that encourage trafficking in women and girls for prostitution and other forms of commercialized sex, forced marriages and forced labour; called on those states to increase cooperation and concerted action by all relevant law enforcement authorities with a view to dismantling trafficking networks; called on those states to allocate resources to programs for healing and rehabilitation into society of victims, including through job training, legal assistance and confidential health care; called on those states to develop education and training programs and policies and consider enacting legislation to prevent sex tourism and trafficking; invited governments to develop manuals for the training of personnel who receive and/or hold in temporary custody victims of trafficking to sensitize them to the needs of victims; and, noted with appreciation the reports of the SR on violence against women and the SR on the sale of children, child prostitution and child pornography and encouraged them to continue to address the problem of trafficking.

**Integration of Women's Human Rights**

The resolution on the integration of women's human rights throughout the UN system (1997/43), *inter alia*: Reaffirmed that discrimination based on sex is contrary to the UN Charter, the Universal Declaration, the Women's Convention and other international human rights instruments; emphasized the role of the Commission on the Status of Women in promoting equality between women and men; referred to the Beijing Declaration and Platform for Action and called on all bodies, organs and agencies of the UN, including the High Commissioner for Human Rights and the High Commissioner for Refugees, to give full, equal and sustained attention to women's human rights in exercise of their respective mandates; reiterated the need for states and relevant UN bodies to include in human rights education activities information on women's human rights; expressed concern that implementation of the recommendations in the concluding documents of the world conferences in Vienna and Beijing remains far from the objectives set out; called for an intensified effort to integrate women's human rights into the mainstream of the UN system; encouraged efforts by the High Commissioner for Human Rights to coordinate activities of relevant UN entities dealing with human rights in considering violations of women's human rights; welcomed the High Commissioner's intention to undertake a comprehensive review of the technical cooperation program from a gender perspective; encouraged strengthening cooperation among all human rights treaty bodies, special rapporteurs, special procedures and other human rights mechanisms of the Commission and Sub-Commission and requested that they regularly and systematically take a gender perspective into account in implementation of their mandates; welcomed the paper prepared by UNIFEM for the meeting of rapporteurs, representatives, experts and chairpersons of working groups (May 1996) and the description of gender-specific reporting and analysis included in that paper; called for further strengthening of cooperation between the Commission on Human Rights and the Commission on the Status of Women and between the Centre for Human Rights and the Division for the Advancement of Women and, in terms of the latter, to ensure that a joint work plan reflects all aspects of work under way and identifies where obstacles and impediments exist as well as areas for further collaboration; requested that this joint plan of work be made available to the 1998 sessions of the Commission on Human Rights and the Commission on the Status of Women; drew attention to the need to develop practical strategies to implement recommendations made by the expert group meeting on guidelines for integration of a gender perspective into human rights activities and programs; welcomed efforts of the treaty bodies to monitor more effectively women's human rights; affirmed that it is the responsibility of all treaty bodies to integrate a gender perspective into their work-including use of guidelines in reviewing states parties reports, development of a common strategy towards mainstreaming women's human rights in their work, incorporation of gender analysis and exchange of information in development of general comments and recommendations with a view to preparation of general comments reflecting a gender perspective and incorporation of a gender perspective into concluding observations; urged states to limit the extent of reservations to the Women's Convention and regularly review reservations with a view to withdrawing them; urged relevant UN entities to provide training on women's human rights to all personnel and staff; drew attention to the need to give consideration to the human rights of women and girls in preparations for the five-year review of the Vienna Declaration and Programme of Action; and, renewed the call to the

High Commissioner for Human Rights to ensure the availability of expertise on gender issues to advise the Office of the High Commissioner for Human Rights, and will consider the question at its 1998 session.

**Traditional practices affecting the health of women and children**

The Sub-Commission appointed a special rapporteur in 1994 to study the issue of traditional practices affecting the health of women and children. At its 1997 session, the Commission on Human Rights endorsed the decision of the Sub-Commission to extend the Special Rapporteur's mandate for two years to allow the SR to follow up and monitor developments related to this question. The SR's reports to the 1997 Sub-Commission (E/CN.4/Sub.2/1997/10, E/CN.4/Sub.2/1997/10/Add.1) summarize replies received from and information provided by governments, UN agencies and organs and a number of non-governmental organizations. The Special Rapporteur's final report will be submitted to the 1998 session of the Sub-Commission.

**Committee on the Elimination of Discrimination Against Women (CEDAW), General Recommendation No. 23 (1997), Political and Public Life (Articles 7 & 8)**

At its 16th session, CEDAW adopted Recommendation 23 on Political and Public Life. The recommendation recalls that, under the Convention, State parties shall take all appropriate measures to eliminate discrimination against women in the political and public life of the country and, in particular, shall ensure to women, on equal terms with men, the right (in article 7): (a) To vote in all elections and public referenda and to be eligible for election to all publicly elected bodies; (b) To participate in the formulation of government policy and the implementation thereof and to hold public office and perform all public functions at all levels of government; and (c) To participate in non-governmental organizations and associations concerned with the public and political life of the country.

In this context, CEDAW comments: public and private spheres of human activity have always been considered distinct; invariably, women have been assigned to the private or domestic sphere, associated with reproduction and the raising of children, and in all societies these activities have been treated as inferior; by contrast, public life, which is respected and honoured, has historically been dominated by men; despite women's central role in sustaining the family and society and their contribution to development, women have been excluded from political life and the decision-making process, particularly in times of crisis; this exclusion has silenced women's voices and rendered invisible their contribution and experience; in all nations, the most significant factors inhibiting women's ability to participate in public life have been the cultural framework of values and religious beliefs, the lack of services, and men's failure to share the tasks associated with the organization of the household and with the care and raising of children.

CEDAW also looks at article 8, which requires that State parties shall take all appropriate measures to ensure to women, on equal terms with men and without discrimination, the opportunity to represent their governments at the international level and to participate in the world of international organizations. CEDAW notes: it is evident that women are grossly under-represented in the diplomatic and foreign services of most governments, and particularly at the highest ranks; many permanent missions to the United Nations and to other international organizations have no women among their diplomats and very few at senior levels; and the situation is similar at expert meetings and conferences that establish international and global goals, agendas and priorities. Yet globalization of the contemporary world makes the inclusion of women and their participation in international organizations, on equal terms with men, increasingly important; the integration of a gender perspective and women's human rights into the agenda of all international bodies is a government imperative.

In the light of this, CEDAW makes, *inter alia,* the following recommendations:

With respect to Articles 7 and 8:

▸ States parties should ensure that their constitutions and legislation comply with the principles of the Convention, and in particular with articles 7 and 8.

▸ States parties are under an obligation to take all appropriate measures, including the enactment of appropriate legislation, to ensure that organizations such as political parties and trade unions do not discriminate against women and respect the principles contained in article 7 and 8.

▸ States parties should identify and implement temporary special measures to ensure the equal representation of women in all fields covered by article 7 and 8.

▸ States parties should explain the reason for, and effect of, any reservations to article 7 or 8; keep the necessity for such reservations under close review; and, in their reports, include a timetable for their removal.

With respect to Article 7:

▸ On the right to vote and stand for election, CEDAW recommends identifying, implementing and monitoring measures to: achieve a balance between men and women holding publicly elected positions; ensure that women understand their right to vote and how to exercise it; ensure that barriers to equality are overcome, including those resulting from illiteracy, poverty and impediments to women's freedom of movement; and assist women experiencing such disadvantages to exercise the right to vote and be elected.

▸ On participation in the formulation of government policy, CEDAW recommends measures to ensure: equality of representation of women in the formulation of government policy; women's enjoyment in practice of the equal right to hold public office; and recruiting processes directed at women are open and subject to appeal;

▸ On the right to participate in non-governmental organizations (NGOs) and associations, CEDAW recommends measures designed to: ensure that effective legislation is enacted prohibiting discrimination against women; and encourage NGOs and public and political associations to adopt strategies that encourage women's representation and participation in their work.

With respect to Article 8:

▸ CEDAW recommends that measures which should be identified, implemented and monitored, should include those designed to ensure a better gender balance in membership of all United Nations bodies, including the Main Committee of the General Assembly, the Economic and Social Council and expert bodies, including treaty bodies, and in appointments to independent working groups or as country or special rapporteurs.

There are also recommendations with respect to States reports under articles 7 and 8.

# *Additional Thematic Approaches*

## Mandates of the Secretary-General

There are seven thematic mandates which are entrusted to the Secretary-General. These mandates are:

- cooperation with representatives of UN human rights bodies;

- human rights and forensic science;

- the protection and promotion of fundamental human rights and freedoms in the context of HIV/AIDS;

- the question of enforced or involuntary disappearances;

- the rape and abuse of women in the areas of armed conflict in the former Yugoslavia, particularly in Bosnia and Herzegovina;

- human rights and terrorism; and,

- human rights and thematic procedures.

## Studies of the Sub-Commission

The Sub-Commission on Prevention of Discrimination and Protection of Minorities maintains a roster of thematic studies, reports and working papers. Three studies were concluded in 1997: impunity and economic, social and cultural rights, prepared by Mr. El-Hadji Guissé (E/CN.4/Sub.2/1997/8); impunity and civil and political rights, prepared by Mr. Louis Joinet (E/CN/4/Sub.2/1997/20); and the human rights dimensions of population transfer, prepared by Mr. Awn Al-Khasawneh (E/CN/4/Sub.2/1997/23; resolution 1997/29).

As of 7 February 1998, the list of ongoing studies, reports or working papers included the following subjects (the date in square brackets indicates the expected date of completion):

- **human rights and income distribution,** [Mr. José Bengoa, 1998] (E/CN.4/Sub.2/1997/9; resolution 1997/107);

- **traditional practices affecting the health of women and children,** [Mrs. Halima Embarek Warzazi, 1998] (E/CN.4/Sub.2/1997/10; E/CN.4/Sub.2/1997/10, Add.1; resolution 1997/8)

- **systematic rape and sexual slavery during armed conflict,** [being completed by Ms. Gay J. McDougall, 1998] (resolution 1997/114);

- **treaties, agreements and other constructive arrangements between states and indigenous populations** [Mr. Alfonso Martínez, 1998] (decision 1997/110);

- **indigenous peoples and their relationship to land,** [Ms. Erica-Irene A. Daes, 1998] (E/CN.4/Sub.2/1997/17 and Corr.1; resolution 1997/12);

- **human rights and states of emergency** [Mr. Leandro Despouy, annual; the 1998 report is being prepared by the new SR on the question of human rights and states of emergency, Mr. Ioan Maxim] (E/CN.4/Sub.2/1997/19; E/CN.4/Sub.2/1997/19, Add.1; resolution 1997/27);

- **the concept of affirmative action,** [Mr. Marc Bossuyt, 1998] (decision 1997/118);

- **article 7 of the Convention on the Elimination of All Forms of Racial Discrimination**, related to teaching, education, culture and information to combat prejudices leading to racial discrimination [Mr. José Bengoa and Mr. Mustapha Mehedi, 1998];

- **the right to education,** [Mr. Mustapha Mehedi, 1998] (resolution 1997/7);

- **the relationship between the enjoyment of human rights and the working methods and activities of transnational corporations** [Mr. El-Hadji Guissé, 1998] (resolution 1997/11);

- **the right of access to drinking water supply and sanitation services,** [Mr. El-Hadji Guissé, 1998] (resolution 1997/18);

- **the right to adequate food as a human right,** [Mr. Asjborn Eide , 1998, update] (resolution 1997/108)

- **juvenile justice,** [Ms. Lucy Gwanmesia, 1998] (resolution 1927/25)

- **weapons of mass destruction or with indiscriminate effect; illicit transfer of arms,** [Ms. Forero Ucros, 1998] (resolutions 1997/36; 1997/37);

- **privatization of prisons,** [Mr. Ali Khan, 2000] (resolution 1997/26);

- **freedom of movement,** [Mr. Volodymyr Boutkevitch, 2001] (resolution 1997/30);

▸ **human rights and terrorism,** [Ms. Kalliopi K. Koufa, 2000] (E/CN.4/Sub.2/1997/28; resolution 1997/39); and,

▸ **human rights and scientific progress,** [Mr. Osman El-Haffé, 2000] (resolution 1997/42).

# Draft Declarations and Draft Optional Protocols

There are, at present, initiatives in progress focused on the elaboration of either draft declarations on human rights or optional protocols to the human rights treaties. These groups are as follows:

▸ The Committee on Economic, Social and Cultural Rights, optional protocol to the Covenant, (E/CN.4/1997/105).

▸ Working Group on an optional protocol to the Convention on the Elimination of All Forms of Discrimination against Women, (E/CN.6/1997/WG/L.3 and E/CN.6/1997/WG/L.3.1).

▸ Working Group on an optional protocol to the Convention against Torture (E/CN.4/1997/33). The 6th session of the WG took place in Geneva, 13–24 October 1997.

▸ Working Group on an optional protocol to the Convention on the Rights of the Child, related to children in armed conflict, (E/CN.4/1997/96).

▸ Working Group on an optional protocol to the Convention on the Rights of the Child, related to the sale of children (E/CN.4/1997/97).

▸ Working Group on the drafting of a declaration on the right and responsibility of individuals, viz. the rights of human rights defenders (E/CN.4/1997/92).

▸ Working Group on indigenous issues, related to the drafting of a declaration on the rights of indigenous peoples (E/CN.4/1997/102). The 3rd session of the WG took place in Geneva, 27 October to 7 November 1997.

# Appendix 1
# METHODOLOGICAL AND TECHNICAL ISSUES

Section A of this Appendix discusses the format of this report and the methodology used to compile the information. Section B contains descriptions of bodies, procedures and terminology used but not defined in *For the Record 1997*.

## Section A.  Format and Methodology

### 1.  Presentation of the Material

This report is a pilot project for what we hope will become an annual report. The time-period covered by *For the Record 1997* is the calendar year, from 1 January to 31 December, 1997. The focus is on the main bodies that take action in the area of human rights. In concrete terms, this means that we cover the work of the Commission on Human Rights in March/April, the Sub-Commission in August, ECOSOC in July, the Third Committee of the General Assembly in November, the sessions of the treaty-bodies whenever they meet throughout the year, and actions or decisions of the Security Council and UN field presences whenever these are relevant. In future years, we hope to expand the coverage to encompass the work of other bodies and agencies in the UN system. However, for this initial report, we have focused narrowly on the major areas of activity.

It is important to stress that, while we have had to summarize actions and decisions of UN bodies and mechanisms, we have striven to present the material as objectively as possible, and with no editorial comment.

The report has been produced in three separate formats in both English and French: in hardcopy (6 volumes); on the World Wide Web at http://www.hri.ca/fortherecord1997, with full hyperlinks to almost all the original documentation for the English version; and as a CD-ROM of the Website.

In this pilot issue, we were not able to provide hyperlinks to the French documents because we were unable to obtain electronic versions of many of those documents from either the Website of the Office of the UN High Commissioner for Human Rights or from the United Nations Optical Disk System (ODS). The ODS currently serves as an archive of all public UN documentation in all official languages since the early 1990s; however, the archive is still very incomplete with respect to languages other than English. This situation may change in the future as the Office of the High Commissioner is making a concerted effort to develop the French and Spanish versions of its Website. Where there are no hyperlinks to English documents, it is because we were unable to locate an electronic version of the document by January 31, 1998, the

cut-off date we had established for accumulating 1997 documents.

When you click on a hyperlink on the Website, you are brought to the top of the document and should use the "find" command in the edit menu of your Web browser to locate a specific country, subject or paragraph within the document. In both hardcopy and on the Web we specify, where possible, not only the UN document number but the relevant paragraphs in the document. Unfortunately, there are many documents in which not all paragraphs are numbered consecutively.

### 2. The Geographic Volumes, 2-6.

In preparing the main section of this report (volumes 2-6), we divided the world into five broad regions which, with one exception, follow geographic lines: Africa (53 entries), Asia (57), Latin America and the Caribbean (33) and Eastern Europe (22). The fifth grouping, Western Europe and Other (29), includes the countries of Western Europe, Canada, the United States, Australia and New Zealand. In the geographic volumes, we have include not only States, but also territories which have ratified at least one of the six major international human rights conventions, and one area (Palestine) which has its own political authority and is the subject of several UN reports and resolutions.

For every geographic entry, the following format was used, although not every entry has information under each heading or sub-heading:

**Date of admission to the United Nations.**

**Treaties and Reports to Treaty Bodies:**

(a) **Land and People:** the report indicates whether or not the country/territory has submitted a "core document" (intended to provide general background information for all the treaty bodies) to the UN. If so, a brief summary of document is provided which focuses on how the government describes its national institutions and procedures for the protection of human rights..

(b) **Reports to treaty-bodies**

1.  "Economic, Social and Cultural Rights" refers to the International Covenant on Economic, Social and Cultural Rights, which entered into force 3 January 1976.

2.  "Civil and Political Rights" refers to the International Covenant on Civil and Political Rights (ICCPR), which entered into force on 23 March 1976.

(i) Optional Protocol to the ICCPR, entered into force 23 March 1976

(ii) Second Optional Protocol to the ICCPR, aiming at the abolition of the death penalty, entered into force 11 July 1991.

3. International Convention on the Elimination of All Forms of Racial Discrimination, which entered into force 4 January 1969.

4. Convention on the Elimination of All Forms of Discrimination against Women, which entered into force 3 September 1981.

5. Convention against Torture and Other Cruel, Inhuman or Degrading Treatment or Punishment, entered into force 26 June 1987.

6. Convention on the Rights of the Child, entered into force 2 September 1990.

With respect to each convention and/or optional protocol that the country/territory has adhered to, the report provides:

▸ the dates of ratification, accession, seccession or signature;

▸ the due date of the next report;

▸ the date when the next report is scheduled to be considered by the relevant treaty-body; and/or

▸ a listing of overdue reports not yet received.

The report also indicates whether the State party has made any reservations or declarations to these instruments. In addition, for every State party report that a treaty-body reviewed in calendar year 1997, there is a summary of the subjects which the governments addressed and a summary of the concerns, comments and recommendations of the treaty-body.

**(c) Commission on Human Rights (CHR):**

**Country Rapporteurs:** If there is a Special Rapporteur, Special Representative or Expert for the country in question, the report of that mechanism is the first to be discussed.

**Resolutions of the Commission on Human Rights:** If the CHR has adopted a country resolution, or if there is a Chairman's Statement on that country, that resolution/statement is summarized.

**Thematic Reports**, organized under three sub-headings:

(i) **Mechanisms of the Commission on Human Rights:** here, we summarize any substantive comments made by the thematic rapporteurs or working groups of the CHR concerning that country; the thematic mechanisms are listed in alphabetical order.

(ii) **Mechanisms and Reports of the Sub-Commission:** here we summarize any substantive comments made by Sub-Commission Rapporteurs or special reports of the Sub-Commission.

(iii) **Other Reports:** summarizes additional thematic reports including those of the Secretary-General and the High Commissioner on Human Rights to the CHR.

**(d) Sub-Commission on Prevention of Discrimination and Protection of Minorities:**

This section summarizes any country-specific resolutions of the Sub-Commission.

**(e) Economic and Social Council (ECOSOC):**

This section summarizes any reports to ECOSOC, including those of the Secretary-General, as well as any relevant resolutions adopted by ECOSOC.

**(f) General Assembly (GA):**

This section summarizes any reports to the GA including those of Special Rapporteurs, Representatives or Working Group, as well as any resolutions adopted by the GA.

**(g) Security Council (SC):**

This section summarizes any relevant reports to the SC including reports of the Secretary-General or statements by the President of the SC, and relevant resolutions.

**(h) UN Field Operations:**

This section summarizes any relevant reports emanating from UN field offices and/or operations.

**Appendix.** Each geographic volume also contains, as an appendix, the reporting schedule of the treaty-bodies, to the extent that it has been established, for all countries in the region.

## 3. Volume 1.
## Thematic Mechanisms and Reports

As explained in the introduction, Volume 1 is devoted primarily to a summary of the work of the thematic mechanisms and related reports presented to the CHR, Sub-Commission, ECOSOC, GA and SC, as well as resolutions of these bodies. Also included, where relevant, are General Comments or General Recommendations of the treaty-bodies on specific issues. The subjects are alphabetically ordered.

Since it has not been possible to be totally comprehensive in the discussion of thematics, we include — under the heading "Additional Thematic Approaches" — information under three sub-headings:

(a) Mandates of the Secretary-General;

(b) Studies of the Sub-Commission, both those concluded in 1997 and those ongoing; and

(c) Draft Declarations and Draft Optional Protocols which are currently being elaborated.

## Section B.
## Bodies, Procedures and Terminology

This section is intended to provide very brief descriptions of bodies, procedures and terminology used throughout this report. The terms are listed alphabetically. As well, each volume contains a glossary of acronyms commonly used throughout the report.

**1503 Procedure:** ECOSOC Resolution 1503 (1970) authorized the Sub-Commission on Discrimination and Protection of Minorities to appoint a working group (i.e., the Working Group on Communications) to consider all communications received by the United Nations "with a view to bringing to the attention of the Sub-Commission those communications, together with replies of Governments, if any, which appear to reveal a consistent pattern of gross and reliably-attested violations of human rights and fundamental freedoms." Under the 1503 procedure, the deliberations of the WG which makes recommendations to the Sub-Commission, the deliberations of the Sub-Commission which makes recommendations to the Commission, and the deliberations of the CHR, which makes recommendations to ECOSOC are all confidential. However, the Commission publicly announces the names of the countries which it is considering under 1503, as well as countries dropped from this list. Governments often go to great lengths to avoid being put on this "black list" of gross violators.

**Accession:** See *Ratification*.

**Commission on Human Rights (CHR):** a functional commission of the Economic and Social Council (ECOSOC), established in 1945 in accordance with article 68 of the United Nations Charter. The CHR, currently comprised of 53 member States, meets annually for a six week session (in March/April) in Geneva. The CHR has played a major role in setting international human rights standards by drafting the International Bill of Human Rights, and many other seminal UN conventions and declarations. The Commission also monitors the implementation of human rights standards and, for this purpose, it has developed a complex system of thematic and country-specific mechanisms, including special rapporteurs and representatives, working groups, and independent experts. In recent years, it has also set up several funds to assist victims of human rights abuses. Non-governmental organizations in consultative status with ECOSOC may attend sessions of the CHR and make written or oral interventions.

**Committee Against Torture (CAT):** one of six treaty bodies, the CAT is comprised of 10 experts mandated to oversee the implementation of the Convention Against Torture and Other Cruel, Inhuman or Degrading Treatment or Punishment, which entered into force on 26 June 1987. States parties which have ratified the Convention are required to submit reports to the Committee every four years on the measures they have taken towards its implementation. Members of CAT review these reports and engage in a dialogue with representatives of the States parties before presenting CAT's concluding observations. As well, CAT considers communications from or on behalf of individuals claiming to be victims of torture, and may consider communications from one State claiming that another is not fulfilling its obligations under the Convention. The Committee may make confidential inquiries into reliably-attested practices of torture in States, and it has developed an urgent action procedure to respond to cases where individuals are under threat of torture.

**Committee on Economic, Social and Cultural Rights (CESCR)** was created in May 1985 by a resolution of ECOSOC to monitor the effective implementation of the International Covenant on Economic, Social and Cultural Rights, which entered into force in 3 January 1976. CESCR is comprised of 18 independent experts who are elected for four year terms. The Committee meets twice a year in three week sessions in Geneva to examine reports of States parties on the action they have taken and the progress made towards the full enjoyment of the rights contained in the Covenant. As well, the Committee has held general discussions on specific human rights concerns and written General Comments which serve as jurisprudential statements interpreting articles of the Covenant.

**Committee on the Elimination of All Forms of Discrimination Against Women (CEDAW)** was created to monitor implementation of the Convention on the Elimination of All Forms of Discrimination Against Women which was adopted 1979 by the General Assembly and entered into force on 3 September 1981. CEDAW, which meets twice a year for two week sessions in New York, is composed of 23 women, experts in the field of their work, elected by the States parties. CEDAW is mandated to examine periodic reports that States parties to the Convention are required to submit every four years, on the legal, judicial and policy measures taken and on the actual situation of the process of fully integrating women in the political, economic, social and cultural areas of their society. The Committee offers suggestions and makes recommendations to States parties based on their discussions with government representatives. Recently, CERD also began issuing General Comments interpreting the content of articles of the Convention.

**Committee on the Elimination of Racial Discrimination (CERD)** monitors the implementation of the International Convention on the Elimination of All Form of Discrimination which entered into force on 4 January 1969. CERD, comprised of 18 independent experts who serve for four year terms, meets twice a year for sessions of three weeks. CERD's members examine the periodic reports States parties are required to make every two years, and issue comments and recommendations on the basis of their diaogue with government representatives. In addition, CERD may not receive, study and give following to individual and State complaints alleging non-respect of the obligations set by the Convention by a State party to that Convention. CERD is also designated to monitors the aim of the Convention regarding Non-Self-Governing Territories.

**Committee on the Rights of the Child (CRC):** CRC, composed of 10 experts who serve in their individual capacity, monitors the effective implementation by States parties of the rights set out in the Convention of the Rights of the Child. The Convention was adopted unanimously by the General Assembly on 20 November 1989 and entered into force on 2 September 1990. This convention is the one which has the largest number of ratifications; only two States (USA and Somalia) have not yet ratified. States parties to the

Convention submit periodic reports to the CRC every five years. In addition to reviewing these reports with the governments concerned, the CRC interprets substantive articles of the Convention; it also devotes a day from its sessional meetings to a general discussion of specific issues. In 1997, the discussion focused on the rights of children with disabilities.

**Core document:** See *Land and People.*

**Declaration:** A declaration is a statement made upon becoming a State party to an agreement. In certain treaties, States parties can make declarations whereby they recognize the competence of a committee to hear and review complaints.

**Declaration under Article 21 of the *Convention Against Torture*** means that the State party recognizes the competence of the Committee Against Torture (CAT) to receive and consider communications by a State party claiming that another State party is not fulfilling its obligations under the Convention. The Committee will only consider complaints if they are: (a) made by States parties that have made declarations under Article 21, and (b) made about States parties which have made declarations under Article 21.

**Declaration under Article 22 of the *Convention Against Torture*** means that the State party recognizes the competence of the Committee to receive and consider communications from or on behalf of individuals who claim that a State party has violated their rights under the Convention. The Committee only considers complaints against States parties which have made a declaration under Article 22.

**Declaration under Article 41 of the *International Covenant on Civil and Political Rights (ICCPR):*** When a State party makes a declaration under Article 41 of the ICCPR, it recognizes the competence of the Human Rights Committee to receive and consider communications by States parties claiming that another State party is not fulfilling its obligations under the Covenant. The Committee will only consider a complaint if: (a) it is submitted by a State party which has made a declaration under Article 41; and (b) the complaint concerns a State party which has made a declaration under Article 41.

**Declaration under Article 14 of the *Convention on the Elimination of All Forms of Racial Discrimination:*** When a State party makes such a declaration under Article 14, it means that the State Party recognizes the competence of the Committee on the Elimination of Racial Discrimination (CERD) to receive and consider communications from individuals or groups within its jurisdiction who claim that a State party has violated their rights under the Convention. The Committee will only consider complaints against those States parties that have made declarations under Article 14.

**General Assembly (GA) and its Third Committee:** The General Assembly is the main deliberative organ of the United Nations. It is composed of representatives of all Member States, each of which has one vote. Because of the large number of questions it is called on to consider, the Assembly allocates most questions to its six Main Committees. These Committees then draft resolutions and submit them to the General Assembly for approval. The Third Committee of the General Assembly, also called the Social, Humanitarian and Cultural Committee, is the Committee which most often addresses human rights questions.

**Human Rights Committee (HRC):** HRC, one of the six treaty-bodies, was established under article 28 of the Covenant on Civil and Political Rights. The Covenant was adopted by the General Assembly on 16 December 1966 and entered into force 23 March 1976. The Committee, comprised of 18 independent experts, meets three times a year for three-week long sessions. The mandate of the HRC is to monitor the effective implementation of the Covenant and of its two optional protocols. The First Protocol, which was adopted and entered into force at the same time as the Covenant, allows individuals to submit complaints against a State party alleging violations of human rights or fundamental freedoms protected by the Covenant. The Second Protocol, which was adopted on 15 December 1989 and entered into force on 11 July 1991, seeks the abolition of death penalty. The Committee examines reports which States parties are required to submit every five years describing the measures they have adopted to ensure respect of the human rights included in the Covenant and the Protocols; it makes recommendations to States parties based on their reports; and it issues General Comments interpreting articles of the Covenant. The HRC also examines individual complaints made under the First Optional Protocol.

**International Bill of Human Rights:** The term is used to refer to articles in the United Nations Charter which make reference to human rights, the Universal Declaration of Human Rights (UDHR), the International Covenant on Economic, Social and Cultural Rights, and the International Covenant on Civil and Political Rights and its Optional Protocols.

**Land and People or the core document:** To facilitate the reporting process for States parties to international human rights instruments, the treaty-bodies have prepared consolidated guidelines for the development of a "core document" or country profile. The document is also referred to as "Land and people", the title of the first section of the core document.

**Office of the High Commissioner for Human Rights (HCHR):** The Office of the HCHR is the UN office with principal responsibility for UN human rights activities under the direction and authority of the Secretary-General. The post of HCHR was established by General Assembly resolution 48/141 of 20 December 1993, after the idea was strongly endorsed in the Vienna Declaration and Programme of Action of the World Conference on Human Rights (Vienna, June 1993). In September 1997, in the context of the programme for reform of the United Nations, the Office of the HCHR and the Centre for Human Rights (formerly the Geneva secretariat for the UN's human rights procedures and machinery) were consolidated into a single Office. The mandate of the Office of the UN HCHR is to: (a) promote universal enjoyment of all human rights by giving practical effect to the will and resolve of the world community as expressed by the United Nations; (b) play the leading role on human rights issues and emphasize the importance of human rights at the international and national levels; (c) promote international cooperation for human rights; (d) stimulate and coordinate action for human rights throughout the United Nations system; (e) promote universal ratification and implementation of international standards; (f) assist in the development of new norms; (g) support human rights organs and treaty monitoring bodies; (h) respond to serious violations of human rights; (i) undertake preventive human rights action; (j) promote the establishment of national human rights infrastructures; (k) undertake human rights field activities and operations; and (l) provide education, information advisory services and technical assistance in the field of human rights.

**Ratification, accession** and **succession** are all terms that indicate that a State has formally become a State party to a treaty. The primary difference in these three terms has to do with the way that the treaty has been approved. **Ratification** indicates that the treaty has been approved by a State's governing bodies. A State is not bound by a convention that it has signed but not ratified. **Accession** means simply that a State has agreed to be bound by the terms of the treaty. **Succession** means that a newly-formed State has agreed to inherit the treaty obligations of its predecessor. For example, when Czechoslovakia ceased to exist, its successor States, the Czech Republic and Slovakia, each succeeded to the human rights treaties that Czechoslovakia had ratified earlier.

**Reservation:** A reservation is a unilateral statement formally made by a State upon signing, ratifying or acceding to an agreement. A State makes a reservation when it intends to modify or limit the effect of certain treaty provisions on that particular State. For example, a State may ratify a treaty but also say that it refuses to be bound by a specific provision in that treaty.

**Security Council (SC):** one of the six major organs of the UN, with the primary function of maintaining international peace and security. Currently, membership in the SC comprises 15 member States, five of which (China, France, Russia, United Kingdom and United States) are permanent members and have veto power. In recent years, as the link between human rights violations and violent conflict has been unequivocably established, the SC has become increasingly concerned with matters of human rights. For example, it was the Security Council which established the ad hoc International Criminal Tribunals on former Yugoslavia and Rwanda.

**State Party:** A State party to a treaty is a State which has formally consented to be bound by the terms of the treaty.

**Sub-Commission on the Prevention of Discrimination and Protection of Minorities:**

established in 1946 as a subsidiary body of the Commission on Human Rights. It is currently comprised of 26 independent experts nominated by Member States and elected by the Commission for a period of four years. The Sub-Commission meets annually for four weeks in August in Geneva. Its mandate permits the Sub-Commission to consider country situations, propose standards and conduct studies on human rights issues. The Sub-Commission presently has four Working Groups; each meets, generally for a week, before the annual session of the Sub-Commission. Working Group on Communications meets in closed session to make recommendations to the Sub-Commission on the confidential 1503 procedure. The other three Working Groups are on Indigenous Populations, Contemporary Forms of Slavery, and Minorities. The Sub-Commission and the latter three Working Groups are open to NGOs in consultative status with ECOSOC, whose representatives may attend meetings and make oral or written statements.

**Succession:** See *Ratification.*

**Third Committee:** See *General Assembly.*

**Treaty-body:** Each of the six major human rights treaties reviewed in this report have established a committee of independent experts (i.e., a treaty-body) mandated to receive and review reports from States parties concerning their efforts to implement their treaty obligations under the convention.

# Appendix 2
# Human Rights Mandates

The mandates of the Special Mechanisms of the Commission on Human Rights and the dates when these mandates will be up for renewal.

## THEMATIC

**Working Group** . . . . . . . . . . . . . . . . . . . . . . . . . . . . . . . . . . . . . . . . . . . . . . . . . . . . . . Mandate Ends

on Enforced or Involuntary Disappearances (5 independent experts) . . . . . . . . . . . . . . . . . . . . . . . . 1998

on Arbitrary Detention (5 independent experts). . . . . . . . . . . . . . . . . . . . . . . . . . . . . . . . . . . . . . . . 2000

## Special Rapporteur or Special Representative

Extrajudicial, Summary or Arbitrary Execution. . . . . . . . . . . . . . . . . . . . . . . . . . . . . . . . . . . . . . . . 1998

Independence of Judges and Lawyers. . . . . . . . . . . . . . . . . . . . . . . . . . . . . . . . . . . . . . . . . . . . . . . 2000

Torture and Other Cruel, Inhuman or Degrading Treatment . . . . . . . . . . . . . . . . . . . . . . . . . . . . . . . 1998

Internally Displaced Persons . . . . . . . . . . . . . . . . . . . . . . . . . . . . . . . . . . . . . . . . . . . . . . . . . . . . . 1998

Religious Intolerance . . . . . . . . . . . . . . . . . . . . . . . . . . . . . . . . . . . . . . . . . . . . . . . . . . . . . . . . . . 1998

Use of Mercenaries as a Means of Impeding the Exercise of the Right of Peoples to Self-Determination . . . . . . . . . 1998

Freedom of Opinion and Expression . . . . . . . . . . . . . . . . . . . . . . . . . . . . . . . . . . . . . . . . . . . . . . . 1999

Racism, Racial Discrimination and Xenophobia . . . . . . . . . . . . . . . . . . . . . . . . . . . . . . . . . . . . . . . 1999

Sale of Children, Child Prostitution and Child Pornography . . . . . . . . . . . . . . . . . . . . . . . . . . . . . . . 1998

Elimination of Violence Against Women. . . . . . . . . . . . . . . . . . . . . . . . . . . . . . . . . . . . . . . . . . . . . 2000

Effects of Toxic and Dangerous Products on Enjoyment of Human Rights . . . . . . . . . . . . . . . . . . . . . 1998

Protection of Children Affected by Armed Conflict. . . . . . . . . . . . . . . . . . . . . . . . . . . . . . . . . . . . . . 2000

## COUNTRY MANDATES DURING 1997

### Special Rapporteurs, Special Representatives or Independent Experts

These mandates are renewed on an annual basis

Afghanistan

Burundi

Cambodia

Cuba

Equatorial Guinea

Former Yugoslavia

Haiti

Iraq

Islamic Republic of Iran

Myanmar

Nigeria

Palestinian Territories Occupied Since 1967

Rwanda

Somalia

Sudan

Zaire (Democratic Republic of the Congo)

# Appendix 3

## Human Rights Treaty Bodies

## Draft Schedules for Consideration of State Reports

The following schedules of the treaty bodies was prepared after the country profiles were completed. This accounts for any discrepancies that may appear between information in the profiles, related to consideration of state reports, and the information contained below. Please note: the following schedule was compiled at the beginning of February 1998 and is subject to change at short notice.

## Committee on Economic, Social and Cultural Rights (CESCR)

*18th Session: 27 April-15 May 1998*

| | | |
|---|---|---|
| Cyprus | 3rd periodic report | E/1994/104/Add.12 |
| Netherlands | 2nd periodic report | E/1990/6/Add.11 |
| Netherlands Antilles | 2nd periodic report | E/1990/6/Add.12 |
| Netherlands: Aruba | 2nd periodic report | E/1990/6/Add.13 |
| Nigeria | Initial report | E/1990/5/Add.31 |
| Poland | 3rd periodic report | E/1994/104/Add.13 |
| Solomon Islands | Non-reporting state | |
| Sri Lanka | Initial report | E/1990/5/Add.32 |

*19th Session: 16 Nov.-4 December 1998*

| | | |
|---|---|---|
| Canada | 3rd periodic report | E/1994/104/Add.17 |
| Germany | 3rd periodic report | E/1994/104/Add.14 |
| Israel | Initial report | E/1990/5/Add.39 |
| Switzerland | Initial report | E/1990/5/Add.33 |
| Tunisia | 2nd periodic report | E/1990/6/Add.14 |

*20th Session: 26 April-14 May 1999*

| | | |
|---|---|---|
| Bulgaria | 3rd periodic report | E/1994/104/Add.16 |
| Cameroon | Initial report | E/1990/5/Add.35 |
| Denmark | 3rd periodic report | E/1994/104/Add.15 |
| Ireland | Initial report | E/1990/5/Add.34 |
| Iceland | 2nd periodic report | E/1990/6/Add.15 |

*21st Session: 15 Nov.-3 December 1999*

| | | |
|---|---|---|
| Argentina | 2nd periodic report | E/1990/6/Add.16 |
| Italy | 3rd periodic report | E/1994/104/Add.19 |
| Mexico | 3rd periodic report | E/1994/104/Add.18 |
| Armenia | Initial Report | E/1990/5/Add.36 |
| Georgia | Initial Report | E/1990/5/Add.37 |

## Human Rights Committee (HRC or CCPR)

*62nd Session: 23 March-9 April 1998*

| | | |
|---|---|---|
| Cyprus | 3rd periodic report | CCPR/C/94/Add.1 |
| Ecuador | 4th periodic report | CCPR/C/84/Add.6 |
| Finland | 4th periodic report | CCPR/C/95/Add.6 |
| Uruguay | 4th periodic report | CCPR/C/95/Add.9 |
| Zimbabwe | Initial report | CCPR/C/74/Add.3 |

# Committee on the Elimination of Racial Discrimination (CERD)

*52nd Session: 2-20 March 1998*

| | | |
|---|---|---|
| Antigua & Barbuda | Without report | |
| Armenia | Initial & 2nd periodic reports | CERD/C/289/Add.2 |
| Bahrain | Without report | |
| Bangladesh | Without report | |
| Bosnia/Herzegovina | Without report | |
| Cambodia | 2nd–7th periodic reports | CERD/C/292/Add.2 |
| Cameroon | 10th–13th periodic reports | CERD/C/298/Add.3 |
| Congo | Without report | |
| Congo DR | Without report | |
| Costa Rica | Without report | |
| Czech Republic | Initial & 2nd periodic reports | CERD/C/289/Add.1 |
| Ghana | Without report | |
| Haiti | Without report | |
| Israel | 7th – 9th periodic reports | CERD/C/294/Add.1 |
| Lebanon | 6th – 13th periodic reports | CERD/C/298/Add.2 |
| Libya | 11th–14th periodic reports | CERD/C/299/Add.13 |
| Mauritania | Without report | |
| Netherlands | 10th–13th periodic reports | CERD/C/319/Add.2 |
| Papua New Guinea | Without report | |
| Portugal | Without report | |
| Russia | 14th periodic report | CERD/C/299/Add.15 |
| Rwanda | Without report | |
| Saint Lucia | Without report | |
| Switzerland | Initial report | CERD/C/270/Add.1 |
| Syria | Without report | |
| Ukraine | 13th & 14th periodic reports | CERD/C/299/Add.14 |
| Uruguay | Without report | |
| Yugoslavia | 11th–14th periodic reports | CERD/C/299/Add.17 |

# Committee on the Elimination of Discrimination against Women (CEDAW)

*18th Session: 19 Jan.-6 February 1998*

| | | |
|---|---|---|
| Azerbaijan | Initial report | CEDAW/C/AZE/1 |
| Bulgaria | 2nd & 3rd periodic reports | CEDAW/C/BGR/2-3 |
| Croatia | Initial report | CEDAW/C/CRO/1 |
| Czech Republic | Initial report | CEDAW/C/CZE/1 |
| Dominican Republic | 4th periodic report | CEDAW/C/DOM/2-3&4 |
| Indonesia | 2nd & 3rd periodic reports | CEDAW/C/IND/2-3 |
| Mexico | 3rd & 4th periodic reports | CEDAW/C/MEX/3-4 |
| Zimbabwe | Initial | CEDAW/C/ZWE/1 |

*19th Session: 22 June-10 July 1998*

| | | |
|---|---|---|
| Belarus | 3rd periodic report | CEDAW/C/BLR/3 |
| Belize | Initial and 2nd periodic reports | CEDAW/C/BLZ/1-2 |
| Equatorial Guinea | 2nd & 3rd periodic reports | CEDAW/C/GNQ/2-3 |
| Nigeria | 2nd & 3rd periodic reports | CEDAW/C/NGA/2-3 |
| Panama | 2nd & 3rd periodic reports | CEDAW/C/PAN/2-3 |
| Peru | 3rd & 4th periodic reports | CEDAW/C/PER/3-4 |
| South Korea | 3rd periodic report | CEDAW/C/KOR/3 |
| Tanzania | 2nd & 3rd periodic reports | CEDAW/C/TZA/2-3 |
| United Kingdom | 3rd periodic report | CEDAW/C/UK/3 |

| *20<sup>th</sup> Session: 19 Jan.-6 February 1999* | Austria | 3<sup>rd</sup> & 4<sup>th</sup> periodic reports | CEDAW/C/AUT/3-4 |
|---|---|---|---|
| | Egypt | 3<sup>rd</sup> periodic report | CEDAW/C/EGY/3 |
| | Finland | 3<sup>rd</sup> periodic report | CEDAW/C/FIN/3 |
| | Greece | 2<sup>nd</sup> & 3<sup>rd</sup> periodic reports | CEDAW/C/GRC/2-3 |
| | Spain | 3<sup>rd</sup> periodic report | CEDAW/C/ESP/3 |
| | Thailand | 2<sup>nd</sup> & 3<sup>rd</sup> periodic reports | CEDAW/C/THA/2-3 |

# Committee against Torture (CAT)

| *Scheduled for consideration in 1998* | France | 2<sup>nd</sup> periodic report | CAT/C/17/Add.18 |
|---|---|---|---|
| | Germany | 2<sup>nd</sup> periodic report | CAT/C/29/Add.2 |
| | Guatemala | 2<sup>nd</sup> periodic report | CAT/C/29/Add.3 |
| | Israel | | |
| | Panama | 3<sup>rd</sup> periodic report | CAT/C/34/Add.9 |
| | New Zealand | 2<sup>nd</sup> periodic report | CAT/C/29/Add.4 |
| | Norway | 3<sup>rd</sup> periodic report | CAT/C/34/Add.8 |

# Committee on the Rights of the Child (CRC)

| *17<sup>th</sup> Session: 5-23 January 1998* | Ireland | Initial report | CRC/C/11/Add.12 |
|---|---|---|---|
| | Libya | Initial report | CRC/C/28/Add.6 |
| | Micronesia | Initial report | CRC/C/28/Add.5 |
| | | | |
| *18<sup>th</sup> Session: 19 May-5 June 1998* | Fiji | Initial report | CRC/C/28/Add.7 |
| | Hungary | Initial report | CRC/C/8/Add.34 |
| | Japan | Initial report | CRC/C/41/Add.1 |
| | Luxembourg | Initial report | CRC/C/41/Add.2 |
| | Maldives | Initial report | CRC/C/8/Add.3 |
| | North Korea | Initial report | CRC/C/3/Add.41 |
| | | | |
| *19<sup>th</sup> Session: 21 Sept.-9 October 1998* | Bolivia | 2<sup>nd</sup> periodic report | CRC/C/65/Add.1 |
| | Ecuador | Initial report | CRC/C/3/Add.44 |
| | Iraq | 2<sup>nd</sup> periodic report | CRC/C/41/Add.3 |
| | Kuwait | Initial report | CRC/C/8/Add.35 |
| | Sweden | Initial report | CRC/C/65/Add.3 |
| | Thailand | Initial report | CRC/C/11/Add.3 |
| | | | |
| *20<sup>th</sup> Session: January 1999* | Austria | Initial report | CRC/C/11/Add.14 |
| | Barbados | Initial report | CRC/C/3/Add.45 |
| | Belize | Initial report | CRC/C/3/Add.46 |
| | Chad | Initial report | CRC/C/3/Add.50 |
| | Guinea | Initial report | CRC/C/3/Add.8 |
| | Honduras | 2<sup>nd</sup> periodic report | CRC/C/65/Add.2 |
| | Yemen | 2<sup>nd</sup> periodic report | CRC/C/70/Add.1 |
| | | | |
| *21<sup>st</sup> Session: May/June 1999* | Armenia | Initial report | CRC/C/28/Add.9 |
| | Benin | Initial report | CRC/C/3/Add.52 |
| | Macedonia | Initial report | CRC/C/8/Add.36 |
| | Nicaragua | 2<sup>nd</sup> periodic report | CRC/C/65/Add.4 |
| | Russia | 2<sup>nd</sup> periodic report | CRC/C/65/Add.5 |
| | St. Kitts & Nevis | Initial report | CRC/C/3/Add.51 |
| | Vanuatu | Initial report | CRC/C/28/Add.8 |

*22nd Session: September/October 1999*

India . . . . . . . . . . . . . . . . . Initial report . . . . . . . . . . . . . . CRC/C/28/Add.10

Mali . . . . . . . . . . . . . . . . . Initial report . . . . . . . . . . . . . . CRC/C/3/Add.53

Georgia . . . . . . . . . . . . . . . Initial report . . . . . . . . . . . . . . CRC/C/41/Add.4

Grenada . . . . . . . . . . . . . . . Initial report . . . . . . . . . . . . . . CRC/C/3/Add.55

Mexico . . . . . . . . . . . . . . . 2nd periodic report . . . . . . . . . . CRC/C/65/Add.6

Netherlands . . . . . . . . . . . . Initial report . . . . . . . . . . . . . . CRC/C/51/Add.1

Venezuela . . . . . . . . . . . . . Initial report . . . . . . . . . . . . . . CRC/C/3/Add.54

*23rd Session: January 2000*

Cambodia . . . . . . . . . . . . . Initial report . . . . . . . . . . . . . . CRC/C/11/Add.16

Iran . . . . . . . . . . . . . . . . . . Initial report . . . . . . . . . . . . . . CRC/C/41/Add.5

Malta . . . . . . . . . . . . . . . . . Initial report . . . . . . . . . . . . . . CRC/C/3/Add.56

South Africa . . . . . . . . . . . Initial report . . . . . . . . . . . . . . CRC/C/51/Add.1

# Index